Georga

MW01122485

Exploration of Rem~ ____ ~ ~ ~.~..~.~.,~.~.~tive
Experience for Young Adults

Georgane Callaizakis-Higgins

Exploration of Remorse as a Transformative Experience for Young Adults

Restorative Justice and Homeless Youth

VDM Verlag Dr. Müller

Abstract

REMORSE IN THE CONTEXT OF RESTORATIVE JUSTICE:
THE EXPERIENCE OF AT-RISK ADOLESCENTS AGED 18 THROUGH 21

Within the criminal justice system, programs in restorative justice hold great promise where punitive regimes often fall short, but remorse appears to be a key element in their success. This study explored the experience of remorse for a particular population of at-risk adolescents aged 18 through 21. Five-hundred and three clients of Urban Peak Denver, an agency serving homeless and runaway youth, constituted the primary population. From this group, 32 participants were recruited for a pilot study through community announcements that sought youth aged 18 through 21 who could read and comprehend English. Since a direct measure of remorse was not available, the TOSCA-A, which measures guilt-proneness, a related construct, was administered. Nine participants with high guilt-proneness scores participated in three focus groups of three participants each. Results showed that one group emphasized the cognitive experience of remorse; another the physical experience; and the third, personality transformation. Forty-five adolescents participated in the formal master study, in which they completed the TOSCA-A. Two high guilt-proneness and two low guilt-proneness focus groups were held, each with three participants. A key finding was while high guilt-proneness groups could remain on topic and talk about their experience of remorse, low guilt-proneness groups had difficulty remaining focused, using humor as a distraction or simply stating remorse was too painful to discuss. Based on the ability to reflect on their capacity for remorse, four individual case studies were then presented for more in-depth analysis, one from each focus group. A version of the TAT was administered to each of these participants, along with structured interviews. The study argued qualitative methods were more revealing in the experience of remorse than quantitative measures, particularly in this age group. Results suggested remorse can give these youth hope and be a catalyst for transformation in their lives. Regarding programs in restorative justice in general, the study concluded that remorse plays a necessary role where offenders are able to own and demonstrate an understanding of the impact of their actions on both self and others. Relationships can then be constructively developed between perpetrator and victim, leading to forgiveness and even transformation.

v

ACKNOWLEDGMENTS

My heartfelt gratitude goes to Urban Peak Denver Staff for their assistance and support and particularly to Jamie Van Leeuwen, Associate Executive Director of Urban Peak Denver and Dr. Carrie Merscham, who provided input on the Thematic Apperception Test analysis. Additionally, I extend my gratitude to both Dr. June Price-Tangney who suggested using the TOSCA-A guilt-proneness scale and assisted with modifying the questionnaire and to Dr. David Harder for making the Personal Feelings Questionnaire - - 2 available for this study. I am deeply grateful to my daughters, Jody and Cassidy Higgins, who tolerated numerous hours while I focused on this endeavor and who still offered their support and encouragement. I thank Dr. Eugene Taylor, my Advisor and dissertation Chair, who was invaluable in helping to articulate this topic that pulls from my diverse areas of interest and experience and Dr. David Lukoff and Dr. Robert Flax for their support as faculty and on my dissertation committee. Most of all, I am deeply touched by and thankful to Urban Peak Denver's courageous youth, particularly those who honored me with their time and stories.

TABLE OF CONTENTS

LIST OF TABLES

ix

LIST OF FIGURES

CHAPTER 1. REMORSE IN THE CONTEXT OF RESTORATIVE JUSTICE

There are few moments more touching than when a grief stricken mother of a dead teenage girl opens her heart to forgive that girl's distraught and remorseful friend who is responsible for the auto accident that resulted in this loss. This was the gift Darlene Linnebur gave to herself and to her daughter's young friend, Heather Clark, thus assisting them to move along a path of healing (Sanchez, 2005). Likewise, a dentist in Tampa Bay, Florida was convicted of murder, at least in part, because his lack of remorse made his story less credible (Goffard, 2002). A San Francisco dog owner would not have faced murder charges "if she had only shown some remorse" (Gould, 2002, ¶ 1). And an additional nine months was added to a Canadian cabinet member's sentence due to his "stubborn lack of remorse" (Bell, 2004, ¶ 1). Restorative justice[1] holds promise for making examples like the first one more common in how criminal justice handles crimes where cost to human lives far exceeds any possibility of material remuneration. It offers potential for healing and reparation of harm to individuals and to humanity. Clearly, the above examples show remorse is something societies look for after commission of a crime. Through research of the literature and from direct experience with processes of restorative justice, this author found remorse is a key element in restorative justice.

Interestingly, while remorse may strongly influence course and outcome of a case in the legal system, this system provides little guidance on assessing the expression of remorse by offenders. Karen (2001) suggests genuine expression of remorse is critical for forgiveness "because remorse softens our hatred and victimization and helps remind us that the wrongdoer is a fellow creature" (¶ 7). Movies such as *Dead Man Walking* and the story of Karla Faye

---

[1] Restorative justice is a process in which those responsible for committing some harm have the opportunity to meet with those affected by the harm. Generally, all parties express their perspective of and feelings about the situation and discuss, with the intention of coming to an agreement, reparative actions that may be taken by those that did the harm.

Tucker demonstrate this particularly well. These stories of remorseful individuals who have committed heinous crimes show how society wrestles with remorse; we value it, and yet do not trust it. It comes after the fact, after harm was inflicted, and, therefore, it is difficult to discern sincerity in its expression (Sarat, 1999) and if it will result in a real change of behavior. Nevertheless, if offenders access feelings of remorse, the belief is they are more likely to successfully reintegrate into society.

Restorative justice offers an opportunity for offenders, who have committed a crime, to become involved in reparation for what they have done. Through this, it also helps facilitate reintegration of offenders into the community in a constructive future role. In general practice of restorative justice, offenders are expected to demonstrate remorse in order to be considered good candidates for this practice. Though remorse is only vaguely defined, judges and practitioners of restorative justice are asked to assess its presence, or potential presence, in offenders. Appropriate demonstration of remorse is believed to signal that offenders have gained, or are capable of gaining, understanding of the impact of their criminal actions. Additionally, some believe that remorse can have transformational power and, in that, can far exceed the practical purpose of bringing offenders back into line with social norms. In light of the following: 1) remorse and restorative justice are intimately related; 2) processes of restorative justice, particularly in Western countries, most frequently involve adolescent offenders; 3) there is little guidance on assessing remorse; and 4) there is little understanding of what the experience of remorse is for populations that are expected to demonstrate it, the principal investigator believes exploration in this area offers a valuable contribution.

3

Purpose

While restorative justice is used most often in juvenile courts with younger adolescents because there is belief that they are less entrenched in negative behaviors and have more potential for change, this author's experience is that there is potential benefit for older adolescents as well. The population of youth[2] for this study will come from an agency in Denver that offers shelter and other services (e.g. education, therapy, employment counseling, etc.) to homeless and runaway youth in the metro area. A large number (43%) of adolescents in the subject population have already been involved in the criminal justice system. Most likely, many first became involved at the level of juvenile courts. They are at-risk adolescents who are likely candidates for the process of restorative justice. Many also have been exposed to the concept of restorative justice in resolving disputes that arise in day-to-day activity at the agency. An overriding benefit of understanding remorse, and also what impedes it, for this population, is that it may be used to help the youth improve their life situations and avoid becoming involved in more serious crimes leading to long-term involvement with the adult criminal justice system.

This study revealed that difficult and challenging experiences of this population affected their experience of remorse. There were differences and similarities between remorse for this population and remorse as discussed in psychological and philosophical literature. This sometimes included diminished capacity to access remorse. It also contributed to previous research by Tangney (1991) and Tangney, Wagner, and Gramzow (1992) and Tangney and Dearing (2002) using the Test for Self-Conscious Affect for Adolescents (TOSCA-A) with different adolescent populations. Differences and similarities between these

---

[2] The term youth is the common term used in these practices, rather than the more scientific term adolescent, which connotes the psychological, physiological, and emotional development of this group. The United Nations General Assembly and the World Congress of Youth delineate this group to include people between 15 and 24 years of age (World Congress of Youth, 2002).

populations and this study's subject population were revealed, including higher scores in shame and lower ones in guilt and pride. Surprisingly, scores for detachment were lower and for externalization were only slightly higher. This study provided further understanding of this population of at-risk adolescents so society can better support and assist them in finding constructive and rewarding roles in their communities. Ultimately, it also contributed to understanding how remorse can operate in the context of restorative justice.

Research Questions

Since remorse is a key element in restorative justice, it is important to understand the experience of remorse for the individuals who are expected to demonstrate it. This study looks at one such population and addresses two questions. The first question is what does an empirical study of remorse disclose about restorative justice? The second question is what is the experience of remorse for the subject population?

To answer these questions, this study explored literature on restorative justice, remorse and apology, law, developmental psychology, and philosophy. It also included an empirical pilot study that provided demographic analysis of a primary population of 503 shelter youth and then drew generalizations about remorse as experienced in small groups of this shelter population. The master study, a more detailed examination, included results from a paper-and-pencil test and qualitative measures of both focus groups and individual case studies. Finally, how these findings relate to restorative justice from the theoretical context of an existential-humanistic and transpersonal perspective is discussed.

CHAPTER 2. RESTORATIVE JUSTICE AND REMORSE

Restorative Justice

Defining restorative justice requires consideration of culture and time period. This concept can also be very narrowly or very broadly defined. Zehr (1990) describes restorative justice as having a very specific vision. He states that:

> Restorative justice sees things differently . . . . Crime is a violation of people and relationships . . . . It creates obligations to make things right. Justice involves the victim, the offender and the community in a search for solutions which promote repair, reconciliation, and reassurance (p. 181).

Some might define it as a process that attends to direct restoration of loss suffered by a victim or group of victims. Others suggest a much broader definition, namely, restoring relationships that have been harmed by crime. Defined even yet more broadly, restorative justice works to repair harm caused by crime (Bazemore & Walgrave, 1999). Defined this broadly, restorative justice encompasses all those who are directly and indirectly harmed by crime, including victims, offenders, families, and community. It can also address issues, such as poverty or discrimination, which may perpetuate harmful behaviors.

While such a broad definition invites inclusion of many consequences that are usually considered restorative, it does not provide enough guidance to assure that practices, such as trying youth in adult courtrooms, are not also labeled as a restorative practice. Marshall (1996) offers a procedural definition in which all stakeholders affected by an offense come together to deal with its results and future implications. This raises many questions such as: Who are the stakeholders? What is it to "deal" with results? Is there a limitation on what can be considered a result of a specific crime? How far into the future do we go? Does this include addressing structural and cultural issues in society? Van Ness et al. (2001) point out that many questions raised may be answered effectively by key principles outlined in Sharpe's

(1998) work. Sharpe took defining restorative justice a step further and suggested five key principles. Summarized, these include: 1) invitation to full participation and consensus; 2) healing what has been hurt; 3) pushing for acceptance of full accountability by the offender directly with harmed parties; 4) reintegration and restoration of relationship so that the words 'victim' and 'offender' may be laid aside as labels of the past, while parties orient themselves toward the future; and 5) provision of an opportunity to look at structural issues, inequities, and injustices that resulted in crime. These key principles honor what is vital in any reparative process. They cover individual accountability, direct contact between victim(s) and offender(s) (allowing them to see each other's humanity), actual restitution, dealing with the past and moving beyond it, and systemic issues that may have led to and continue to perpetuate the problem. These are some of the same key principles that will be discussed in the following review of the historical origin of restorative justice.

A Historical Perspective on Restorative Justice

While restorative justice is considered a relatively new concept in juvenile justice, it actually has a long history ranging back to hunting and gathering cultures. According to Weitekamp (1999), a process very similar to restorative justice was a common way to achieve justice in acephalous societies.[3] People in these societies were closely dependent upon each other, requiring a system of justice that worked to restore victims from harm committed against them and to restore offenders to the society. These societies found that they must somehow restore relationships in order to continue to function in their tightly connected groups. This restoration could involve blood revenge, retribution, ritual satisfaction, or

---

[3] Acephalous societies, in this instance, are defined as societies that are more egalitarian in form, that lack a formal centralized leadership, such as a head of state. This term would include hunting and gathering cultures.

restitution. The last of these was most used because it quickly restored the relationship of the offender with others through repair of harm (Weitekamp, 1999).

Nader and Combs-Schilling (1977) have identified six key factors in processes of restitution in acephalous societies. These are: (1) keeping the situation from escalating into further destructive or disruptive behavior; (2) reintegration of the offender back into the group and avoidance of further stigmatization; (3) taking care of the victim; (4) reiterating the society's values by providing for some form of justice for the victim and offender; (5) further socialization of all members of the group about its norms and values; and (6) providing a method of regulation and deterrence in the daily functioning of the group. Interestingly, these factors are also captured by Sharpe's (1998) key principles. This consistency, this author proposes, points toward important aspects that are common to requirements for a functional society in its efforts to encourage and maintain pro-social behavior. Furthermore, because these aspects are not only identified in early acephalous societies as useful, but are also 'reinvented' in current time in Western culture by Sharpe (1998), it suggests that they are not limited by time or culture.

An important part of the process, and the first key factor mentioned by Nader and Combs-Schilling (1977), was first to provide some distance between victim and offender, and allow for a cooling off period. This often involved allowing the offender to seek sanctuary so that the victim(s) would not retaliate. Their second key factor, reintegration, is vital to allowing society to resume smooth functioning. Reintegration not only prevents isolation and further negative relations, but also pulls the offender back into conformance with cultural norms. It helps to allay fears of other members of society around further crimes committed by the offender and allows anger that naturally arises to be defused. According to Sarat (1999), one of the strongest driving forces for angry revenge against offenders is actually society's fear of its vulnerability to commission of such acts.

This approach in acephalous societies indicated a mentality in the community that there was not just one person who was responsible for deviant behavior. Rather, deviant behavior was the responsibility of the community and it was both a problem for the community and a failing on the part of the community (Weitekamp, 1999). In contrast, we might say that this sense of community is hard to find in today's developed world. Paradoxically, with globalization has also come a segregation of the individual. We can sit at home and at one level be totally disconnected while connecting intellectually and technologically to far-reaching parts of the world. Meanwhile, connectivity between families is less and less the case. This makes a sense of community more difficult to discern in a society where the traditional community is seen as interconnections between families. Groups of people that might make up a community are so dispersed that use of the term community becomes unlikely. People in general, and youth in particular, are at a loss for roles as contributing members. Bazemore (1999) suggests that this sense of a valuable contribution to community is what aids youth in growing out of delinquency. Further, instead of viewing youth as contributors, society views them as non-contributors who must be provided for and are separate from contributing adults. This then disconnects young people from opportunities for meaningful relationship with real-life adult role models. Early communities did not have to contend with segregation of the individual and loss of valued roles for youth, because survival of the community was dependent upon each able-bodied person performing a vital role.

Restorative processes are not limited to acephalous societies. There is also indication that they were used in early state societies. The term 'state societies' refers to societies that have some form of centralized governance, in contrast with more egalitarian cultures. In early Hebrew, Anglo-Saxon, and Turkish societies, among others, laws were often written in a way that required restitution both for property and personal crimes (Weitekamp, 1999). Laws set payment for personal crimes leading to death or personal injuries. Sometimes these were set to very specific details such as loss of a tooth or finger, etc. In the event of death, there was also a set way of making payment to family members for their loss. If there were no family members, payment would then go to the state or royal treasury. In some instances, if the offender refused to make payment, any member of the society could kill the offender without penalty. The primary purpose of these laws, however, was to avoid blood feuds (Weitekamp, 1999).

As western societies continued to move away from acephalous forms and toward that of a formal head of state, individual victim's rights were eroded, and injury to the state became the dominant concern. Resolution of conflict increasingly became a duty of the head of the state, rather than of the community and parties who were directly involved or suffered the loss. With this increasing transfer of responsibility, it also became more common that repayment for offenses was made to the state rather than to victims.

Restorative Justice Today Compared with Mainstream Justice Systems

Restorative justice takes a variety of forms in Western civilization. In the U.S. and Europe, it primarily takes shape as victim-offender mediation[4] in the juvenile justice system.

---

[4] Victim-offender mediation most commonly involves the offender(s), victim(s) directly affected by the offense, and one or more mediators who facilitate the meeting. Generally, meetings are held separately with the parties to assure their readiness for the process prior to the meeting between all parties. The meeting with all parties usually starts with the offender acknowledging what he or she has done and what led up to commission of the criminal act. The victim then has the opportunity to voice thoughts, feelings, and questions. Then an agreement for restitution may be written.

In Australia, New Zealand, and Canada restorative justice encompasses a more varied approach, including practices associated with indigenous Aboriginal groups. Gradually, this variety of practices is being integrated into justice systems in the U.S. and Europe. Some such practices include introduction of family group conferencing and conferencing circles. Group conferencing most commonly follows a format similar to victim-offender mediation, using group consensus to develop a restitution agreement (Van Ness et al., 2001). Family group conferencing has evolved in New Zealand as a simulation of indigenous practices of the Maori people (Blagg, 1997; Van Ness et al., 2001). This is referred to as the Wagga Model. This practice has been adapted into many different formats, but generally involves friends and family members of the victim and offender who care about one of the two and have in some way been affected by the crime. Conferencing circles, adapted from First Nations practices in Canada, expand the circle of participation to include members of the criminal justice system and other community members who believe they have been affected by the crime (Van Ness et al., 2001). Still another form of restorative justice is a process implemented through the South African Truth and Reconciliation Commission. This commission is a forum in which victims and offenders come forward and tell the stories of how they were harmed or of crimes they have committed during the apartheid conflicts of South Africa (Scheper-Hughes, 1999).

Interestingly, this expansion of the types of restorative practices comes at a time when the overall trend is in the direction of a more punitive attitude toward offenders. Bazemore (1999) suggests that the frustration over rehabilitative efforts that are perceived as having not worked to reform offenders is causing the pendulum to swing to a more punitive attitude. In crime, victims usually become dehumanized in the eyes of the offenders and, through this, the relationship between victim and offender suffers its greatest harm. In a punitive approach, by

11

requiring offenders to pay for wrongdoing through punishment to some nebulous greater whole, mainstream justice systems not only succeed in dehumanizing offenders, but also succeed in further dehumanizing victims. This approach also prevents any repair of the victim-offender relationship because the victim is often removed from the process, or at the very least focus is on the offender, and the victim is simply a fact in the legal case against the offender. This not only obstructs the re-humanizing of the victim in the offender's eyes, but also in the victim's own eyes.

Regarding offenders, the punitive approach focuses on what is wrong with them, labeling them as such and working to reduce their freedom so society will be protected from them. This places offenders in a position of having no value to society. While focus is on offenders and their punishment, the very nature of this focus both devalues and dehumanizes offenders. According to Bazemore (1999), punitive sanctions may undermine progress toward any reparative and rehabilitative goals. He suggests this is because punishment stigmatizes, humiliates, and isolates offenders within the community. By doing these things it has an opposite effect to what the judicial system may be intending. It also limits the possibility that offenders will gain or regain self-respect in the community. Beyond this, it reinforces offenders's self-focus and may keep offenders from focusing on victims and harm that was caused (Bazemore, 1999). Bazemore extrapolates this to mean that offenders may have a lessening of self-restraint by attenuating natural feelings of guilt and the sense of morality.

By using a restorative approach there is opportunity to re-humanize the victim in the offender's eyes. Through this process, the victim is respected, given back dignity, and empowered with a voice. Similarly, restorative justice re-humanizes the offender by providing him or her with an opportunity to perform some constructive act by working to repair harm that has been done. It extracts something useful from the offender and gives back to the victim(s) and society. This stands in contrast to the punitive system that simultaneously takes freedom from offenders and resources from society as offenders are supported in prison or otherwise.

Among the different approaches, there is one called the balanced approach to restorative justice (BARJ). Moeser (1999) discusses BARJ and provides thoughts on an alternative to either a system focused on punishment or one focused on rehabilitation. BARJ involves three key concepts of community protection, accountability, and competency. This approach is based on an assumption that true safety occurs only when all individuals value and learn to make law-abiding choices. Therefore, any plan that addresses community safety must include both short- and long-term strategies that move youth toward being connected with the community and having necessary skills and interests to become contributing members. Moeser's (1999) thoughts echo the focus of restorative processes of acephalous societies and Sharpe's (1998) key principles. BARJ moves youth away from what Moeser (1999) calls learned irresponsibility, from which many negative behaviors arise, and toward the kind of competence that generates success, ownership, and recognition in the community. Moeser's (1999) inclusion of competency is similar to Bazemore's (1999) belief that it is important for our youth to feel like valued contributors and, in order for real restoration to occur, they must be assisted in finding a role that allows them to offer a useful contribution.

Another shift occurring is movement toward revitalizing processes of restorative justice of indigenous peoples. The Australian government's response to high crime rates among Aboriginal people is one example of this. Aboriginal people have had the highest crime rate of any group in Australia and have been a continued source of difficulty for their

13

government (Weitekamp, 1999). Recent response has been to introduce a process similar to

what ancestors of the Aboriginal people used to bring justice to their society (Blagg, 1997;

Weitekamp, 1999). This process is similar to conferencing circles.

Forcing a society to assimilate from a perspective that is traditionally restorative in

nature to a mainstream punitive system can seriously impair the society's ability to deal with

criminal behavior among its people. This occurs because the old system is rendered useless,

and yet, the new system does not make sense within their paradigm. Weitekamp (1999)

suggests that this leaves them ill equipped to discourage or bring justice to criminal behavior

within their own group. As an effort to correct this, and to remedy crime rates among

Aboriginal youth, the Australian government has implemented the Wagga Model of New

Zealand in the belief that it will allow the Aboriginal people to handle their own problems

(Weitekamp, 1999). Some proponents of restorative justice question whether or not this is

actually what has occurred (Blagg, 1997). In any event, this too has left the Australian

government and Aboriginal people with some difficulties since the new generation of

Aboriginal people was not taught in the way of the earlier generations. This has resulted in a

need for relearning the old way (Weitekamp, 1999). The Australian government has

responded by involving police as parties responsible for controlling the process. Interestingly,

use of police in this way has drawn the most criticism. Reintroduction of a system that

resembles the process used by ancestors of the Aboriginal people is also criticized as piracy of

the shell of a system for exploitation and Westernization by mainstream Western cultures

(Blagg, 1997). This perspective will be covered more fully in discussion that addresses

cultural and structural issues.[5]

---

[5] Cultural and structural violence are defined as harm that occurs to a group of people due to implicit values in the culture, which often lead to explicit formal structures in society that perpetuate that harm. The beliefs that early settlers held about Native Americans eventually resulted in discriminatory practices and laws regarding this group.

Legal Issues in Restorative Justice

A criticism of restorative justice is that it does not protect the legal rights of the juvenile as effectively as might occur in a courtroom where legal counsel is present to actively represent the client's interests. Van Ness (1999), basing his argument on empirical investigations of the issue of protection of legal rights in the restorative process, counters this criticism. The primary basis for his argument is research performed by Bassiouni (1993). Using 10 international agreements and 139 national constitutions, Bassiouni (1993) determined that there are 11 fundamental rights of accused and convicted individuals. Van Ness (1999) identifies five of these fundamental rights that are most likely to impact youth in the process of restorative justice. These include:

1. The right to recognition before the law and equal protection under the law;
2. The right to freedom from torture and cruel, inhuman and degrading treatment or punishment;
3. The right to presumed innocence;
4. The right to a fair trial; and
5. The right to assistance of counsel. (pp. 266-269)

The first of these rights is concerned with assuring a discrimination-free process. Frequently, victim-offender mediation is led by and involves individuals who are Caucasian. Looking more closely at this, Van Ness (1999) points out that these programs are most often implemented in areas that are predominantly Caucasian. It appears then, that whoever is able to access this process is subject to bias toward Caucasians. In addition to racial concerns, another possible concern is discrimination based on gender. Van Ness (1999) believes this is particularly true in family conferencing because of the patriarchal nature of the structure of many families. Due to the deliberate informality of the process, discrimination very possibly may influence the outcome.

Studies have been conducted, however, showing that the outcomes of the courtroom and restorative justice are similar regarding gender and race issues (Van Ness, 1999). What this means is that if discrimination is occurring, the two processes appear to be consistent with each other in this respect. Therefore, while there may be a problem, it is most likely not accentuated by using a restorative approach. Van Ness (1999) also points out that advocates of restorative justice may be willing to accept some inconsistencies that could appear discriminatory due to the plurality of cultures and values. In other words, different cultures have different values and some variance in outcome is appropriate due to these differences. This seems an interesting and questionable argument that discounts the possibility of basic morality and reinforces structural and cultural violence. Because it is so, does not make it right. It simply means that insidious permeation of this idea as a cultural norm has allowed it to seem acceptable. While studies so far show that discrimination in restorative justice is no worse than that of mainstream judicial practices, the importance of making this process available to a diverse group of people and also incorporating cultural sensitivity is vital.

The second right, freedom from cruel, inhuman, and degrading treatment or punishment, is particularly relevant concerning the practice of shaming. While Massaro (1991) contends that Americans are particularly averse to contrived shaming practices, this is countered with a reminder that these rights were derived from Bassiouni's (1993) work, which was based on international standards. The topic of shaming will be discussed more fully in the section on cultural and structural issues, but it is important to mention that offenders are believed, at the international level, to have a legal right to be free of degrading treatment. Deliberate shaming potentially violates that freedom.

In addition to more blatant forms of cruel, inhuman, and degrading treatment or punishment, we should also consider unreasonable stipulations in restitution agreements. Regarding this concern, victim-offender mediation implements several checks that are intended to avoid inappropriate penalties and unreasonable agreements. Mediators themselves, as neutral facilitators, must guide parties away from inappropriate agreements for restitution. If the offender is a minor, then the parent must also be included in assuring appropriateness of restitution. If the case has been referred for mediation from the judicial system, then a third checkpoint for avoiding inappropriate restitution is the judge's review of the mediation agreement.

The third right, presumed innocence, may or may not be applicable in processes of restorative justice. Frequently, in victim-offender mediation the case is sent to mediation to work out restitution and the offender's guilt has already been determined. If, however, another accusation arises during mediation, and it becomes part of the restitution agreement, the youth has a right to appeal that agreement in court. Ideally, the mediator or facilitator would remind the youth that he or she has a right to deny guilt and to halt the process if that seems appropriate. If guilt has not been determined before the restorative process, then any resulting agreement must also be subject to appeal.

Considering the fourth right listed by Van Ness (1999), use of the phrase "the right to fair trial" could mean the offender must have an equal opportunity to be heard and to participate in the process. In order for this to occur in restorative practice, he or she must be informed about the process from the start and must not be coerced. This includes a clear explanation of how the process works, ability to halt the process, and the option to resume the court process. It is vital to avoid situations where the youth feels pressured to assume responsibility for something against his or her will, or for something he or she did not do. This situation may occur when the youth either feels pressed by adults or others in authority. It could also occur as a result of the youth wanting to be finished with the process, or feeling that coming to agreement in this process is a better alternative to going to court. This is why it is important for the facilitator to be practiced in identifying these possibilities, and vigilant about addressing them.

The final right identified by Van Ness (1999), assistance of counsel, is perhaps one that can cause the most discomfort for people who are used to having an advocate represent them and handle proceedings. In a restorative process, parties are asked to become vulnerable and speak openly and directly to other participants. Offenders have the most to lose from a legal standpoint. It is important that the offender's attorney understand the process so that he or she can advise the client, but the process itself requires the offender's direct involvement in order for it to be meaningful.

Because restorative justice is more informal and requires direct involvement of parties, rather than professionally trained attorneys, it does risk falling short in due process. This is not, however, inevitable. Further, when restorative processes are run appropriately they respect human rights and dignity, empower participants, and offer opportunities for transformation that might not otherwise be realized. This researcher's perspective is that, ideally, every case is a likely one for processes of restorative justice. Realistically, some cases are better left in the legal system. Perhaps these two systems are at their best when they work hand-in-hand, checking and balancing each other.

Cultural and Structural Issues as They Affect Restorative Justice

This section deals with the very fabric of how a society is structured and how that structure is influenced by cultural attitudes. These attitudes and resulting structures can then have an adverse impact on certain groups of that society. When this occurs, the terms cultural violence and structural violence become applicable. For example, a cultural attitude that a certain group is less adequate in some way results in a cultural norm that prevents them from being seen, or seeing themselves, as equally capable. Eventually, this cultural norm expresses itself structurally as policies or laws that disallow the group, either directly or indirectly, from participating equally in society. In time, while these laws may be seen as discriminatory and be abandoned, they have already placed the group at a disadvantage. Recovery from this disadvantage is difficult because the nature of the culture and structure still carry imprints of the original attitude.

Recognition of the impact of cultural and structural issues on crime, and in turn restorative juvenile justice, is critical for effective solutions to issues of criminal justice. Unwillingness to recognize the impact of cultural and structural issues can in part be explained by a concept coined by Carter (1988, p. 420-421) as "bilateral individualism," or a need to blame a specific individual for wrongdoing that has occurred. Carter portrays this need as based in fear of becoming a victim, or being re-victimized, and hope to alleviate this fear by striking back. This allows people to feel secure in the belief that they have isolated and controlled or eliminated the perceived source of their fear. This might be seen as giving individuals grasped by uncontrollable fear an outlet for rage, allowing them to feel less vulnerable and weak, lessening fear. This rage is not limited to victims. Family, friends, or others with an allegiance to the victim are also likely to feel rage. This may result in desire on their part to also vent anger on the offender.

Additionally, when a crime is committed it is difficult to set aside the offender's choice to act, and to accept that structural or cultural issues are even partially the cause (Van Ness, 1999). If one is able to accept these issues as part of the cause for criminal behavior, then, as a member of the culture or society, one also has to accept some responsibility for the crime. People are often averse to even considering this because it says to the individual and the society that they are not only victims, but may also be, at some level, 'perpetrators' or, in more constructive terms, responsible parties. Ironically, contrary to the belief that finding a scapegoat will alleviate fear, some studies indicate that the restorative process itself can be cathartic and lead to less fear, anxiety, and anger about crime and about the offender (Immarigeon, 1999). Perhaps this is so, at least in part, because when one owns responsibility for a situation, with that ownership there also is possibility of being empowered to do something about the situation.

Nevertheless, in looking at crime and restorative juvenile justice, it would be narrow-sighted to ignore cultural and structural issues. This is so because these issues inevitably influence who is repeatedly involved in the juvenile justice system and why simply implementing mediation or conferencing programs only scratches the surface of the problem of juvenile crime. As will be discussed further in this section, predominantly minorities, particularly African American youth, are the offenders in the juvenile justice system in the U.S. When you look at it from sociological perspective, this is a reflection of underlying cultural and structural issues.

As in the U.S., the inordinate numbers of Aboriginal people involved in the Australian justice system as offenders begs consideration of cultural and structural issues. Blagg (1997) shares an interesting perspective on cultural and structural issues relating to high crime and custody rates for Aboriginal people. In some areas of Australia, the arrest rate for Aborigines is 28 out of 100, and each of these is charged on the average with five offenses. In comparison, statistics from California prisons show that, in 1997, 33% of African American males over 15 years of age were under the supervision of the criminal justice system (Edington, 1997). In Minneapolis, the ratio of African Americans to Whites in prison is 25.09 to 1, while African American representation in this city's general population is only 3.5% (Johnson, 2002). While the statistics are not completely comparable between these cities and Australia, they do demonstrate that both of these groups are seriously over-represented in their respective criminal justice systems.

As discussed earlier, response to the arrest record for Aborigines was implementation of a system of family conferencing using the Wagga Model from New Zealand. The key principle in this system is re-integrative shaming, which, in theory, involves calling upon social disapproval and pangs of conscience in a formal ceremony to deter juveniles from continuing to offend (Braithwaite, 1989). Blagg (1997) contends that the system used in Australia is a one-dimensional interpretation of the system used by the Maori people in New Zealand. In New Zealand, the system has been a method that significantly reduced the power of police. In Australia, police facilitate the process and have the power to implement 'creative' re-integrative shaming plans (Blagg, 1997). According to Young (2001), new legislation has reduced the power of police to punish in moderate offenses. The greater concern, according to Young (2001), is that facilitation by police can make the process seem overly intrusive and like "state inflicted punishment," rather than an agreement by members

of the conferencing circle.

Blagg (1997) uses the term "Orientalism"[6] to label how the concept of family

conferencing has been implemented in Australia. He describes this process as:

> ...Primarily, powerful acts of representation that permit Western/European cultures to contain, homogenize and consume 'other' cultures. It is through such techniques of representation that we identify what is essentially 'knowable' about them: and our knowledge of them then becomes a kind of cultural capital, the accumulation of which serves to reinforce our nascent cultural superiority (Blagg, 1997, p. 3).

Examples of this process can be seen in integration and Westernization of many aspects of

Eastern spiritual practices and Native American customs. While Blagg's comment places a

decidedly negative spin on intent, it is particularly valuable in bringing to awareness that

trying to understand something from the structure of the existing paradigm, rather than

mentally stepping into the phenomenology of what is being studied, bodes ill for essential

understanding of the subject of study. A phenomenological understanding helps to avoid

overlaying the dominant cultural belief system onto the concepts and processes of another

culture or group. This is a particularly valuable understanding in multi-cultural or gender-

based conflicts (Faure, 1995, Lederach, 1992; Kolb & Coolidge, 1991).

Blagg (1997) also looked at the concept of re-integrative shaming and raised valid

questions relating to the Aboriginal people – – questions that may well be applicable to non-

dominant groups in other societies. According to Blagg (1997), the Maori people of New

Zealand have a hierarchical, family-based warrior culture in which shaming is closely linked

to social honor. In contrast, the Aborigines of Australia, it seems, act more as a collective than

a hierarchy. They also have a history of being completely dominated by Caucasian inhabitants

of Australia, similar to that of Native Americans. This domination has included taking

---

[6] This is a term coined by Edward Said in *Orientalism: Western conceptions of the Orient (1995).*

children from their families to place them in domestic service to assimilate them. In some states this is said to have included genocide (Blagg, 1997; Reynolds, 1989). While efforts were made to undo mechanisms that encouraged oppression and disproportionate incarceration of Aboriginal people by police, police are sometimes still stigmatized by involvement in commission of these acts (Blagg, 1997).

The question is two-fold. If police are the main agents of family conferencing, does it not seem like more of the same for Aboriginal people? The second question that arises is, if these are a people for whom social shaming does not hold meaning and who have been denigrated by the ruling culture, how much more shamed can they be, either in the eyes of the dominant culture or in their own? If shame is described as a reaction to tension between ego ideal and actual behavior (Morrison, 1989), Aboriginal people need first to have an ego ideal that matches the dominant culture's expectation and have self-esteem that is high enough to allow for a gap between ideal and actual.

Similarly, if a youth steals food because he or she is homeless and hungry, what is there to take from this youth, except his or her freedom? The ironic truth is that some youth do not mind being arrested, because then they will have access to regular meals. A moment stands out for the author from a conversation with a youth from a homeless shelter. Before coming to the shelter, the youth had been living on top of a school building. When school came back into session, it was time to move and this brought the youth to the shelter. The youth had an outstanding warrant for stealing. When asked about the theft and the reason for it, the youth responded that it was a bag of chips and a drink that was stolen "because I was hungry." This is not an uncommon situation for youth in this shelter. It seems highly improbable that a process of re-integrative shaming would be helpful here. It is a tragedy though that this youth had to steal food to survive. Should the parents or the community be shamed into taking responsibility for this child? Somehow, that does not seem a long-term answer either. Many, if not most, of these types of situations occur because of a deficiency. Making parties feel further deficient will not help them respond with what is needed.

Moeser (1999) suggests that the best crime-prevention is a justice system in which strategies are aimed at "re-weaving the fabric" of family, community, and relationships. Whether the system incorporates victim-offender mediation, family conferencing, conferencing circles, or another form of restorative processes, it must maintain integrity and be seen as a process that truly accomplishes transformation. One part of this transformation that practitioners often look for is a sense of understanding on the offender's part that he or she has done some harm, is willing to be accountable for this harm, and has a sense of how the other might feel – – that there is a sense of remorse.

What This Means for Victims and Offenders

Reasonably, we might ask whether or not victims and offenders see themselves as better off for having participated in a process of restorative justice. Perhaps it is worth a reminder that in restorative justice, a primary concern with the offender's ability to feel remorse is avoiding re-victimization. Studies of victim-offender mediation suggest that in the majority of cases, re-victimization had not occurred. These studies showed that victim satisfaction with the restorative process correlated with effective explanation of the process prior to its start, direct face-to-face contact between victim and offender, and the perception that the process was voluntary (Umbreit, Coates, & Vos, 2001).

Umbreit et al. (2001) look at twenty-seven victim-impact studies that covered programs in the U.S., Canada, England, and Scotland. While most of these programs focused on property crimes and minor personal offenses, some involved serious violent crime, including murder. These studies confirmed that in these mediations the process is highly relational and is much less about agreement for restitution. Findings showed that one of the primary reasons for the victim's participation was to meet the offender face-to-face and to ask questions that assisted him or her in understanding the crime and why he or she was chosen as victim. Additionally, a four-state study indicated that getting repaid for their loss and helping the offender were of equal importance for victims interviewed. Another interesting finding was that reaching and fulfilling an agreement held greater value for victims than the actual restitution. In Canada and England, victims who went through mediation were 50% less likely to express fear of re-victimization than those who had not gone through mediation.

While the focus of restorative justice is and should be the victim, offender outcome is also important to success of the process. This is true from at least three perspectives. The first is that victims are clearly interested in helping the offender. The second is that offender attitude during and after the process clearly affects victim satisfaction. The third is the controversial belief that offenders are often victims as well.

Schiff (1999) examined victim-offender mediation and family conferencing circles to determine offender satisfaction and benefit (e.g. lower rates of recidivism) from restorative processes. Offenders responded more positively to victim sanctions and to being accountable when they believed they had been treated fairly in the process. Research showed that this was more so in mediation than in the mainstream criminal justice system. Similar to the Umbreit et al. (2001) findings on victim response to mediation, face-to-face meetings seemed to have a positive impact on offender satisfaction and to lower rates of recidivism. There was some concern that offenders might feel coerced by the possibility of reduced sentencing; however, limited research indicates that benefits of victim-offender mediation are greater than negative impacts (Schiff, 1999). Research of family group conferencing in New Zealand suggested that this form of restorative practice also resulted in high participant satisfaction, though offender satisfaction tended to be higher than victim satisfaction. Studies in New Zealand and Australia showed that approximately 70% of offenders believed that outcomes were fair. In a U.S. study, while perception of fairness did not differ between the court process and conferencing, offenders who participated in conferencing were more likely than offenders who participated in court processes to believe that they were held accountable (Schiff, 1999). Results of studies on recidivism were inconclusive, but seemed to indicate there was some decrease in recidivism and that, when re-offense occurred, the offense was less serious. Youth also indicated that bringing the family into the process resulted in their feeling more responsive to the family's support of them in not re-offending.

Schneider (1990) reported that incarcerated offenders believed that restitution would have been more punitive than incarceration. Interestingly, offenders who made restitution, as long as it involved face-to-face meetings and some service in addition to payments, found restitution preferable to incarceration. Lower recidivism rates were associated with offenders who had more victim contact. Additionally, they may be related to completion of restitution as a result of offender's internalization of responsibility for their acts.

There is some reason why face-to-face interaction, as occurs in mediation, may yield higher satisfaction levels. Victim-offender mediation, unlike negotiation-based mediation, focuses less on reaching agreement and more on the process itself. The sense of violation that the victim feels, particularly in personal crime, but also in property crimes, requires some reparation. Therefore, it is the relationship that requires repair, and indeed may be the only thing that can be repaired, because the deed has been committed. In the case of more serious crimes, such as those involving death, the harm resulting from the deed might be irremediable. It makes sense then that restorative processes in which victims and offenders come face-to-face are more likely to result in satisfaction for the parties. Scheper-Hughes (1999) tells a story of a case brought to a community Truth and Reconciliation Commission where the offender could not come for himself and sent a representative in his stead. The commission listened to the representative, but postponed the case until the offender could come face-to-face with the victim, community, and commission, thus stressing the importance of this interaction. They also stressed the importance of offenders facing the shame of seeing and being seen by the community while admitting to the crime they committed. This shame is different from contrived shaming punishments, rather it comes from facing those whose opinion one values and accepting accountability for harm one has inflicted. It was a type of shaming that also brought with it a sense of dignity and respect for self and other.

In spite of these encouraging reports, studies discussed here are limited and do not clearly establish a causal relationship between the process of restorative justice and successful outcomes. For example, choice of defendants referred to the program may be an influencing factor on lower rates of recidivism and higher rates of completion of restitution. The selected defendants often are chosen based on the hope that they can be rehabilitated. Use of these processes in more serious offenses would also assist in understanding their value so that a valid comparison can be drawn between serious offenses handled in the mainstream justice system and in the restorative justice system. This could also be said for less serious offenses. Studies that compare courtroom outcomes with outcomes from restorative justice where offenders and situations are similar in both processes would provide more valid conclusions.

While restorative justice is implemented in a variety of ways, depending upon the country, culture, intended purpose, and understanding of what is reparative action, general agreement seems that the offender and the affected party or parties must be directly active in the process, and this is most effectively done face-to-face. This suggests that a critical aspect of restorative justice is about relationship, specifically, restoring relationships (including one's relationship with oneself), helping the victim find a way to move away from relating from a victim role, and reintegrating the offender into the community. To facilitate this, most practices require offenders to demonstrate recognition of what they have done, accountability, and remorse for harm that has been inflicted by their actions. Restorative practices can attempt to accomplish this via different avenues; for example, some enlist shaming and others enlist empowerment. Different cultures support and benefit from different approaches.

While, this author's perspective is that in an ideal world every issue could be handled through a process of restorative justice, such an approach may require a level of cultural understanding that individuals and societies have not reached at this point. This does not mean, however, that a restorative attitude could not be used throughout dealings concerning justice, whether in the mainstream or practices of restorative justice. There is potential benefit from further study and further understanding of use of restorative justice and how it might be integrated into more than just the juvenile justice system.

Remorse

To realize the value of restorative justice, it is important to understand how remorse is used and valued in the legal system. As previously stated, remorse is used extensively in the legal system, but there is very little explanation of how it is defined, how to identify it, and how it is experienced by those who must demonstrate it. This literature review will begin with a review of what is available in legal and restorative justice literature and then turn to

psychological and philosophical literature to help further inform the understanding of

remorse. Sarat (1999) describes remorse as a suitable emotional response to one's

wrongdoing. It is the expected rational response. It does not seem surprising that the legal

system seeks to couch what they consider an emotional response in the context of rationality.

I suggest, as does Bandes (1999), that the legal system attempts to minimize emotion, this

very essential part of being human, in order to maintain its supposed objectivity. Yet, it

pervades the law as an inevitable part of this system that is constructed and administered by

humans with human emotions. From an existential-humanistic and transpersonal perspective,

it is important to consider the whole of what it means to be human – – anything less than this

leaves a system that falls short of its potential. Furthermore, failure to recognize and assure

appropriate use of something as intrinsic as emotion places the system very much at risk of

losing the very objectivity and rationality it attempts to emulate. On this topic, Nussbaum

(2004) states, "If we leave out all the emotional responses that connect us to this world of . . .

external goods, we leave out a great part of our humanity, and a part that lies at the heart of

explaining why we have civil and criminal laws, and what shape they take" (p. 7). Yet, upon

examining the literature and questioning a Douglas County magistrate, there is little specific

guidance regarding remorse. The humanness of remorse as a reaction to one's wrong doing is

appreciated, but the legal framework does not seem to have the capacity to describe human

qualities of this expression. The offender's reward for demonstrating remorse is the possibility

of a reduced level of punishment, as determined by using a very clearly defined point system

(Federal Sentencing Guideline Manual, 2002a).[7]

---

[7] This table has a horizontal axis showing criminal history category from I to VI. Criminal history points given for factors such as repeat offenses determine the category. The vertical axis is the Level and Zone of the offense with increasing severity from 1 to 43. The placement on these two axes is used to determine the length of incarceration ranging from 0 months to life.

Keeva (1999) and Bandes (1999) speak to this apparent failure to incorporate normal human emotions into the legal system. A sincere apology has potential to move a legal case to settlement before it reaches the courtroom (Keeva, 1999). Keeva wonders why apology is such an uncommon occurrence in the legal system, when it can be such a powerful tool in assuaging the hurt of the injured party. Lazare (2004) provides further insight into the value of a well-intended and executed public or private apology. He goes on to provide us with a list of psychological needs of the person who has been harmed and that these needs must be met, either in part or in total, depending upon the circumstances, for an apology to be effectively healing. While Lazare suggests that these are psychological needs, they are undoubtedly interwoven with and based upon the emotional experience of the person who has been offended. Understanding these needs also helps to explain why face-to-face meetings in processes of restorative justice are vital to success of those processes. The needs include: Restoration of self-respect and dignity; assurance that both parties have shared values; assurance that the offenses were not their fault; assurance of safety in their relationships; seeing the offender suffer; reparation for the harm caused by the offense; and having meaningful dialogues with the offender (Lazare, 2004, p. 44). This author suggests that by meeting these psychological needs, an apology can also address and assuage the accompanying emotions. This lends further credence to Bandes's (1999) belief when she points out, "emotion pervades the law" (p. 1), and yet it is traditionally viewed as having a minimal role in conduct of legal business. She seeks to raise awareness about this gap in the legal system, hoping to begin to fill it with her edited collection of essays in *The Passions of the Law* (1999).

30

This effort to remove emotion from law runs counter to importance of remorse in restorative justice, a process which requires participants to show their humanity in order for it to be effective. It seems that desire to eliminate or control the impact of emotions is further reflected by tightening of remorse's influence in criminal justice through formal sentencing guidelines (Sarat, 1999). Paradoxically, sentencing guidelines are set such that failure to show remorse and take responsibility for a criminal act will likely result in a more severe penalty. Evidence of this is in how sentencing levels are set in the Supreme Court Sentencing Guidelines of the United States, New South Wales, and Canada (Endicott, 2001, Federal Sentencing Guideline Manual, 2002b, and Supreme Court New South Wales, 2002). As previously indicated, the U.S. Supreme Court sentencing table is based on a point system that determines the level of a crime. The level of the crime and number of offenses are associated with a range of months of incarceration. If an offender accepts responsibility for a crime and demonstrates remorse, the judge may reduce the level of sentencing by two levels (Federal Sentencing Guideline Manual, 2002b). It is also notable that these guidelines allow for greater consideration of remorse when demonstrated before conviction is imminent or when a person comes forth voluntarily, before he or she is known to have committed a crime. Sentencing guidelines are more lenient for those who turn themselves in before capture. Change of heart becomes ostensibly more believable in this case. It is possible to see this as an initial step toward remorse because it is a movement from being held responsible to accepting responsibility. Experiencing genuine sorrow is the next step. The question is, did the person's coming forward initiate primarily from an intrinsic desire to accept responsibility, or extrinsically from fear of being caught? If it is the latter, experience tells us that likelihood of the individual taking that next step toward feeling genuine sorrow is significantly diminished.

As we can see, remorse has potential for considerable impact on a person's life in the legal system. Not surprisingly, since this literature offers little in the way of defining remorse, it offers even less in how one assesses remorse. Even Sarat's (1999) attempt to elucidate the importance of remorse in the legal system falls short. He offers a description of remorse as "a retrospective embrace, and expression, of allegiance to the existing normative order." He still does not provide guidance in assessing remorse. He also does not provide any suggestion that remorse may lead to a transcendent or transformational experience. His definition simply provides for reinforcement of the norm.

Particularly in juvenile justice, remorse can influence the course and outcome of a case through processes of restorative justice. In fact, restorative justice in the United States has its strongest influence in juvenile justice systems. As discussed previously, in victim-offender mediation, mediators are asked to make a key determination about whether or not offenders feel, or are capable of feeling, remorse for what they have done. Additionally, according to a magistrate in the Jefferson County Juvenile Justice system, the judge's assessment of remorse can also be a determining factor in referral of cases to mediation from the court system. When asked how he assesses remorse, this magistrate stated that experience is his only teacher and guideline for this. He defines remorse as:

> [The] . . . recognition by a defendant of something that they did that was wrong, and a realization of how that action affected this other person, and a realization that was a mistake and they could have done something different. How can they go forward and do something different then, or go forward and do something different now, so that they can change that in the future (personal communication, April 10, 2002).

Recognition, realization, and change are key actions offered by the magistrate's definition. The young person must first have recognition of right and wrong. Then he or she must realize not only how that other person felt, but also that there was a choice. The final part of the definition, change, provides hope of reparation in this situation, or of a new way of doing things in the future so that he or she chooses not to repeat the action.

As the Colorado magistrate shared, beyond life and on-the-job experience, there is no standard, training, or guideline, of which he is aware, that teaches members of the bench to know when a defendant is truly remorseful. When asked if he ever wonders if a youth is merely a good actor when demonstrating remorse, he acknowledges that this is a question he asks himself. To help make this assessment, the magistrate asks several questions of the youth for insight into whether or not he or she understands what it might be like to be in the victim's place as the recipient of harmful action. If the youth has a plan to right the wrong or to assure that he or she does not repeat the mistake, the magistrate views this as an opening for further understanding. He then tries to further the youth's understanding of how the victim may have felt. He may start by having the youth experience some equivalent material loss. The magistrate is attempting to evoke empathy from this youth. He intuitively assumes a relationship between empathy and remorse.

Psychological and Philosophical Perspectives of Remorse

The Role of Empathy and Relatedness in Remorse

When speaking about empathy and the need for the person who has inflicted harm to experience the victim's humanity, Gobodo-Madikizela (2002) offers some insight to remorse demonstrated by perpetrators of apartheid crimes. She brings more depth and breadth to what the magistrate touches upon as he attempts to lead the youth in his courtroom toward empathy. She states:

> When perpetrators experience remorse they are experiencing the pain of their victims – the pain which was inaudible to them when their victims were dehumanized in their perception. Remorse is allowed to come when the perpetrator sees the victim as

human and can experience his or her pain . . . [.] Remorse, therefore, transforms the
image of victim as object to victim as human other (Gobodo-Madikizela, 2002, p. 17).

She also suggests that absence of empathy denies relatedness through our shared humanity

and attacks the very essence of what it is to be human. We act as human beings when our

apology comes from experiencing the pain of true remorse, (Gobodo-Madikizela, 2002).

Shafranske (1989) differentiates levels of relatedness and how remorse would be

experienced at each of these levels. He identifies these levels as somatic, interpersonal, and

ontological. Remorse experienced in the somatic and interpersonal levels is associated with

concepts of object relations. At this level, it is motivated by a threat to the individual's

physical or interpersonal needs and sense of connectedness to the object. A person

experiencing remorse in the ontological context recognizes the wrong that has been

committed as an injury to the very humanness of the world, of which he or she is a part. In

addition to object relations, parallels can be drawn with Maslow's hierarchy of needs and

concepts of self-actualization and metamotivation. Remorse experienced at the somatic level

may be seen as motivated by a perceived or real threat to what Maslow calls physiological

and safety needs. Similarly, remorse experienced at the interpersonal level is based on a threat

of loss in the area of Maslow's love and belongingness and esteem needs. The ontological

level, like the level of Maslow's self-actualizing individuals, requires a leap beyond narrow

self-interest of the individual. The individual transcends the usual perception of the world and,

in Maslow's (1971) words, "the self has enlarged to include aspects of the world and that

therefore the distinction between self and not-self (outside, other) has been transcended" (p.

301). This description is similar to Shafranske's (1989) description of remorse as experienced

at the ontological level.

34

Brothers (1989) proposes a model that represents the relationship of the individual with context, other, and self. She also believes that it is important to distinguish between destructive self-flagellation and Houston's (1987) concept of opening oneself up to "sacred wounding." She interprets "sacred wounding" as one's story in all its pain and glory, as it fits within the larger universe. The three factors she offers in her model appear to correlate, in respective order, with May's description of *Umwelt,* our relationship with the environment around us, *Mitwelt,* our relationships with others, and *Eigenwelt,* our relationship with our self. According to May (1983), healthy people live simultaneously in these three modes. Likewise, Brothers (1989) suggests that relationships with context, self and other must be in balance. If these are out of balance, the individual is more likely to engage in harmful action. When there is balance, it can allow empathy and remorse to arise in an experience of the sacred wounding and transformation. Without balance, one runs the risk of becoming stuck in self-flagellation. May (1983) tells us that without being in the three modes, we cannot truly understand love. Without love, remorse cannot be at its reparative and transformative best. The remorseful person might not be able to avoid the grips of self-flagellation or find forgiveness, either from self or from other.

Relationship between Guilt and Remorse

Tangney and Dearing (2002) suggest a connection between remorse and guilt. Guilt, in their terms, is a moral feeling about a bad behavior, as opposed to shame, which is a feeling that the self is bad. According to Tangney et al. (1992), guilt is often used interchangeably with shame, revealing a confusion of these two constructs, as their studies have defined them. This confusion is important in light of their studies that showed guilt correlated more closely with positive outcomes, while shame more likely correlated with depression,

35

psychopathology, and unconstructive anger. Further, they maintain that these must be viewed as very distinct constructs, and that shame may actually act as an obstacle in moving toward empathy and remorse. Using their TOSCA, they demonstrated that, while there are some connections between the two constructs, they are very clearly different in resulting personality characteristics.

Tomkins (1995), on the other hand, considers the affect of guilt as contained within that of shame, meaning that he believes guilt is a type of shame. In fact, he further suggests that guilt more closely relates to contempt. This strongly contrasts with Tangney et al.'s (1991, 1992, & 2002) presentation of guilt and shame as moral emotions that appear to be on opposite ends of a continuum. In his description of primary affects, Tomkins does not present one that resembles Tangney's description of guilt. Perhaps a resolution of this is that guilt as Tangney defines it is not an emotion, but occurs in a secondary position as cognition. When a person, who is not engulfed in a script of feeling shameful, engages in a harmful act, he or she may first experience a mild form of shame. Due to an overall positive self-esteem, he or she may be able cognitively to move to guilt as defined by Tangney. The emotions involved here may be a complex that could include sadness, compassion, and regret, among others. These feelings may subsequently result in a sense of responsibility for one's actions and remorse. It is possible that Tangney's guilt scale actually indirectly measures self-esteem.

May's (1983) discussion on the concepts of anxiety and guilt as ontological offer yet another perspective on the possible relationship between guilt and remorse. Building upon Kiekegaard's description of anxiety, May proposed that ontological anxiety arises in anticipation of one's potentiality and freedom. If one denies or fails to fulfill this potentiality, ontological guilt results. Ontological anxiety and ontological guilt are at odds within the individual. To reach one's potentiality, one must find courage to face the unknown and to face anxiety associated with it. Tillich (1952) states, "Anxiety strives to become fear, because fear can be met by courage" (p. 39). If courage is not nurtured and developed sufficiently in a child, then ability to tolerate ontological anxiety is seriously impaired (Spencer, 2004) and ontological guilt is more likely to result. It is possible to view ontological guilt as what lies beneath the surface of remorse. Deeply remorseful individuals see that they have failed to live up to a standard. Shafranske (1989) and Shaw (1989) connect remorse with a perceived threat to one's relatedness. This relatedness could be to oneself, to another, to the world, or to some higher power. A threat to these relationships could reasonably be seen as a threat to one's existential being.

It seems that while each author and theorist speaks in different terms about a different aspect of this construct, there is some overlap. For example, in Tangney's terms, shame is a self-deprecating emotion that might equate with Brothers's concept of self-flagellation, while remorse that can stem from guilt, as a more productive emotion, would be more closely aligned with the "sacred wounding" (p. 47). Stern (1989) suggests that guilt and regret are foundations for remorse, but that remorse transcends these foundational emotions. This may lead us to wonder whether or not remorse can simply be categorized as an affect. Perhaps it is more aptly described as a state of being, similar to May's ontological guilt, or possibly a complex, occurring at the level of personality, that comes from interplay of cognition and emotions. These emotions may include shame, sorrow, empathy, compassion, dread, and possibly guilt. If this were so, then it follows there would be considerable variety in the facets of remorse described by each author.

Remorse and Transformation

There is more to remorse, however, than empathy, recognition of the humanity of the other, and understanding of harm one has caused. There is an internal piece, specifically recognition of a standard or barometer that tells the remorseful person that his or her action was unacceptable. If this were not so, then remorse for something that did not involve self or another person would not occur. One would not experience remorse for harm against an entity such as nature or against one's God. This relates to an aspect of remorse that can be transformational and bring the individual to a higher, and yet more internalized, way of being.

Lest this paper appear completely oblivious to opinions that view remorse as a destructive force, rather than an experience with transformational powers, it is important to give voice to that position as well. Greenberg and Fitzpatrick (1989) suggest that regret is an essential ingredient for psychotherapy, in contrast to remorse, which focuses on personal inadequacy. Hauck (1989) sees remorse as wallowing in depression, self-hate, and feelings of inferiority. The basis of differences between those who view remorse as having transformational power and those who see it as unconstructive appears to be one of semantics. These authors may simply be using different names, or one could say that the former is "true remorse" that is based, as Stern (1989) and others suggest, in guilt and regret, and the latter is based in shame. While this still could be considered a matter of semantics, it is interesting to see, as discussed later in this study, how participants in focus groups of the pilot study characterize remorse. They did tend toward a view that remorse is transformational, meaning that somehow consciousness is expanded by insights that have altered their world view. The individual is now different in some way.

Remorse, literally translated, means a biting back, meaning the past comes back to bite a person for what he or she has done. For remorse to have a transformational effect, however, one must also be willing to fully bite into and chew this resurrected piece of history. Jacobsen and Theilgaard (1999) interpret Kierkegaard's philosophical and theological view of man to posit that there are three conditions required to allow for the possibility of remorse. The first condition, freedom of choice means the person must have had the choice to act differently. Secondly, this biting back aspect of remorse must be possible. The element of time must exist for the past to come up in the present and create a painful remembering. The third condition, the need for some meaningful value, requires a sense of harmful action versus helpful action, or good versus evil.

Remorse, even at its transformational best, is inseparable from pain. Kierkegaard's viewpoint on this is that remorse is inevitably accompanied by dread (Jacobsen & Theilgaard, 1999). People predominantly choose a life of lightness, superficiality, and irrelevance over facing the painful side of oneself and one's history. It seems to follow then that if one is going to dull one's senses in order to avoid feeling pain, joy must also be buried, leaving us with triviality and meaninglessness. May (1983) suggests that this rejection of experience "leaves one with the vapid, weak, unreal sense of being" (p. 107). Jacobsen and Theilgaard (1999) point out that Kierkegaard refers to the unconscious with his belief that, in an unguarded moment, one's history, though forgotten, is not lost and will emerge. Kierkegaard placed great importance on knowing and remembering oneself. One must "come to one-self in self knowledge" (Kierkegaard, 1851/1990, p. 105). Being absorbed in knowledge of things outside of oneself is to be "absent from yourself" (Kierkegaard, 1851/1990, p. 105) and, though this might normally be viewed as being sober, Kierkegaard views it as being intoxicated. Moore

(1989) suggests that a deeply remorseful experience can be a form of regression in service of the ego. This means taking a step back by acknowledging and dealing with the past may result in valuable progress and growth. Raising one's awareness so that senses are no longer dulled allows the painful past to emerge. It allows joy that is buried with it to emerge as well. Taking one more step in this understanding, the ability to access remorse then opens access to the depth of life and what is meaningful in each individual's existence. Indeed, assimilation of such insight and experience would be transformational.

An obstacle to transformation, however, can be that one accesses remorse and then becomes neurotically stuck in a place of dwelling upon the irremediable harm and the bad self that committed this harm. This author suggests this is symptomatic of the superficial circumstances that the majority of us choose for our lives. If one truly has a sense of value, the value that Kierkegaard refers to, then it is not necessary to dwell in the hopelessness of feeling worthless. There is still choice, and the person can choose to see his or her own value, despite the evil deed. The offender must acknowledge both the good and the evil as very real parts of the self. Just as the victim must live with the harm that cannot be undone, the offender must live with the dread of what he or she has done.

Moral Development and Remorse

With this potential to fall into the hopelessness of the perception of a bad self, it is reasonable to question whether or not youth, particularly at-risk youth who have little or no life experience of remorse or empathy, have a sense of value of self and other and can fathom how they affected the victim(s). There are numerous perspectives on moral development in psychology and the criminal justice system. One example of work in criminal justice is that of resiliency, particularly as it relates to young offenders's ability to access shame, guilt, empathy, and remorse. Werner and Smith (1992) describe resiliency as the capacity for "self-righting" and for transformation and change.

Vasquez (2000), who works with a juvenile resiliency program in the Ohio State Department of Corrections, suggests that only when youth have begun to fulfill self-esteem needs will they be able to engage in self-reflection and gain access to empathy and remorse. This sequential relationship between esteem needs and remorse suggests a parallel with Maslow's hierarchy of needs. Only once their sense of intrinsic value begins to be established can they become open to their connection with the larger world. This does not suggest that they are now fully self-actualizing individuals. It does suggest that they are on a possible path that can lead to self-actualization, and that it, most likely, is a dynamic back and forth action, depending upon what needs are and are not being met.

The basic premise of resiliency work with at-risk youth is that if they have had some meaningful attachment to another person, there is an untapped reserve of resiliency that can make the difference for youth in turning their lives around and overcoming the negative impact of traumas they have experienced. Shaw's (1989) discussion of the value of relatedness seems to be born out in this study of resiliency. Further, scientific evidence supports a belief that risk factors (such as abuse, neglect, or exposure to drug use) were less important in a youth's life than protective factors (such as supportive adult figures) when predicting the youth's outcome in adult life (Werner & Smith, 1992).

Vasquez's (2000) findings suggest that not only did inmates begin to see their own strengths, but they also began to see strengths of others as well. They began to see the positive side of their humanity and that of others. They saw their mistakes, admitted to them, and took responsibility for them. Building their self-esteem gave them strength to look at these mistakes and experience shame, guilt, and empathy for others without having to fear that it would destroy them. It taught them that, even if they made mistakes, they still had positive attributes and something to offer that allowed them to be valuable contributors. They can choose to see their value and that of others.

Remorse cannot be separated from morality and moral development in the human experience. Generally, moral development is regarded as internalization of society's norms or standards of how we should behave with each other and in our environment (Berk, 1994, p. 475). This is a very narrow definition of moral development, which does not address transcendent experiences, but rather limits existence to the mundane world of what society dictates to us. Interestingly, this is very similar to Sarat's definition of remorse. It is equally as lacking in depth and breadth. Perhaps early childhood moral development does begin with extrinsic motivations such as a parent's approval or disapproval. One would hope that it expands well beyond these limitations.

Piaget (1932/1965) offers some insights into parental, or primary caretaker, influence on early moral development. His work suggests that parental dominance and authoritarianism may hinder the child's ability to develop his or her own moral judgment. It may actually block the child from internalizing family and societal moral beliefs. Clearly, Piaget's work demonstrates a strong parental influence, albeit negative in this instance, on the child's moral development.

This author would argue, as many schools would also argue (e.g. cognitive behavioral, social learning theory, and object relations) that parents strongly influence the initial internal psychic structure with which the youth approach peer interactions. When this structure or system of beliefs answers what the youth sees as his or her needs in the situation, then it is most likely reinforced. When it is not effective with the peer group, then it requires some adjustment. The degree of adjustment is often limited by the initial belief structure itself, particularly if the structure the youth has learned from the parents is overly rigid. Harris (1999) is one who argues that peer influence is stronger than parental influence. I do agree that there is a great deal of learning that occurs when the youth puts his or her understanding of socially acceptable behavior into practice with the peer group, however, parental influence cannot be discounted as the initial influence. Even from an existential-humanistic and transpersonal perspective, parents or primary caretakers are a vital influence as they are the source for providing necessary conditions for optimal growth and realization of the individual child's potential.

Hoffman (2000) approaches parental influence from the viewpoint of how it fosters empathy. He defines empathy as "the spark of human concern for others, the glue that makes social life possible" (p. 3). Hoffman (1998) believes that empathy begins as an automatic response in infants. He bases this on the infant who hears the distressed cry of another infant and, in response, cries in apparent equal distress. He suggests that youth develop their natural tendency toward empathy through a process that begins with disciplinary induction on the part of the primary caretaker. He suggests that if children receive feedback that encourages them to understand how a person they have hurt may feel, their natural inclination toward feeling empathy is fostered and begins to mature. He calls this type of parental guidance inductive discipline.

To elucidate how inductive discipline works, Hoffman (2000) points out several types of discipline that can influence moral development. The first type is when the parent responds to a young child's undesirable behavior in a way that causes the child to feel bad about him or herself for the harmful act. This actually may have a reverse effect on instilling a sense of moral action because the child becomes consumed with either negative self-judgment or with defending against such self-judgment. The second focuses on the action, instead of the child, as bad. It does not have the same potential to be as counterproductive as the first style, because it takes the focus off the child's negative sense of self. The third style, inductive discipline, focuses on the act as bad, how the victim may feel, and the child taking responsibility for that act. The victim becomes salient, thus fostering empathy arousal. In this style of discipline, the caretaker pointedly discusses with the child the feeling that the person they have harmed might experience.

According to Hoffman (2000), this is a critical initial step for the child to make the transition from egocentrism to beginning to take into account the claims of others. He maintains that empathy is the vehicle that carries us to guilt and remorse, and the disciplinary inductions instill empathy. One might reasonably wonder whether or not at-risk adolescents have had much of this type of discipline. This perspective would suggest that youth who have experienced serious abuse early in their lives might have this affective development arrested. Lack of ability to experience true remorse can be both a developmental issue and a defense mechanism that results in blocking the ability to be vulnerable enough to fully experience either one's own pain or that of another. Tangney et al. (1992) correlate this with shame.

According to Kaufman (1985), shame requires a splitting of the self in such a way that the self passes judgment upon itself. Guilt as Tangney et al. (1991, 1992, & 2002) define it, on the other hand, is a judgment of the action of the self. In this case, the self-concept remains unified. Their belief is that the first type of parental discipline described by Hoffman fosters the development of shame, as the child internalizes the parent and becomes his or her own judge. With enough of these shaming incidents of discipline, according to Kaufman (1985), the child's internal view of self will transform from "I feel shame" to "I am shameful." He uses Tomkins's concept of scripts, suggesting that the child begins to link together separate events of shame inducement to create an apparently coherent internal script that confirms, in a self-perpetuating manner, the self as being shameful. Kaufman (1985) points out that this type of punishment of the self by the self, more traditionally, is defined as guilt. This phenomenon, in combination with what Tomkins (1995) calls internalized contempt, can occur secondarily to shame, thus setting the stage for splitting of the self into two parts. Interestingly, shame not only causes one to want to hide oneself from view, shame itself will also hide from view and, instead, may appear as angry aggression or rejection of the person who has shamed the child. Kaufman (1985) further suggests that shame links with affects, drives, and needs and results in these being hidden as well. This means, for example, that a child who has been shamed for being affectionate or fearful may repress these feelings so that there is no conscious awareness of the shame or of the affects. He believes this is particularly true because Western culture tends to consider shame as taboo. This contrasts with Mediterranean or Oriental cultures that organize more openly around shame. Henderson, Zimbardo, and Martinez (2001) have also suggested that in Western culture, shame, shyness, fear, private self-consciousness, and social anxiety become linked together, causing a person to withdraw from a situation, rather than move toward it in reparative action, even if the desire to do so is there.

As stated previously, in contrast to the first type of discipline discussed by Hoffman, the third type of discipline he describes, inductive discipline, helps maintain integrity of the self-concept and focuses on judgment of external action and on empathy toward the injured other. While allowing the self-concept to remain intact, this type of discipline also encourages the child to take responsibility for harmful actions. Beyond comparing this with Tangney's definition of guilt-proneness, a further inference is that children with high guilt-proneness are more likely to experience remorse. This type of discipline can help the self-concept to develop so that it allows the ego to remain soft and flexible, without the need to raise its defenses. Empathic experiencing of the other's pain does not become an attack on the ego's sense of well being, thereby allowing for the possibility of remorse.

Erikson's psychosocial stages also offer insight into the constructs of shame and guilt. In Stage 2, autonomy versus shame, doubt, Erikson (1950/1963/1985) provides a clear sense of the construct of shame, as well as how it might become overwhelming and lead to anger against the judging authority. This description correlates well with how Tangney et al. (1992) define shame and with Kaufman's description of a shame-affect link which may manifest outwardly as anger. It also may be a critical piece in understanding why the youth of interest to this study tend to defy authorities in their lives. Between the ages of three and six the child enters stage three, where he or she is dealing with the issue of initiative versus guilt. If the child becomes too controlled and is not supported in experimentation and exploration (i.e., the developing superego stifles the ego), then a situation of too much guilt results and initiative does not develop appropriately (Erikson, 1950/1963/1985). Using definitions proposed by Tangney et al. (1992), this author suggests that Erikson may have been referring to an overabundance of guilt that may lead to shame, or guilt mixed with shame. Taken in this way, Erikson's theory is helpful in understanding why the population of youth being studied may or may not have moved to a level of feeling remorse for harms they have caused.

Beyond childhood, Tangney's research suggests that certain self-conscious responses continue to develop into adulthood. Specifically, types of situations that young children, adolescents, and adults mention when talking about moral emotions vary with age. Children more frequently mentioned concrete situations such as physically hurting someone or something. Adolescents introduced the concept of feeling guilt for inaction or, suggestive of May's concept of ontological guilt, failure to attain ideals. This is also suggestive of Piaget's concept of moving from concrete operations to formal operations, when adolescents develop abilities of abstract cognition. It further relates with Erikson's stage of Identity versus Identity Diffusion, as adolescents begin to develop personal identity and ideals. Adults were more likely than children to focus on interpersonal aspects, that is, how others viewed them, in relationship to situations involving guilt and pride. This agrees with Erikson's proposition that, during young adulthood, interpersonal relationships grow in importance in the stage of Intimacy versus Isolation.

Closing Thoughts from the Existentialist's Point of View

Ultimately, remorse is not something one would generally seek to experience. Despite this, it is an inevitable characteristic of being human that we engage in behaviors which provide ample opportunity to experience it. A suitable phrase translated by Jacobsen and Theilgaard (1999) from Kierkegaard's original version of *The Concept of Anxiety* aptly summarizes the value of remorse: "for what else is remorse other than that which looks back – although it hastens the movement to what is ahead" (pp. 197-198). A strong theme in much of the discussion in the literature was the power of remorse to evoke positive change. This change can be at the level of a simple behavioral change or it may lead to important life transformation. To be available to this transformation, however, one must also be open to the accompanying pain and dread.

CHAPTER 3. PRELIMINARY EMPIRICAL STUDY

From the existential-humanistic and transpersonal perspective, the underlying epistemology of this study, value lies in seeking understanding of the person as a whole. Therefore, as discussed previously, understanding remorse in the larger context of restorative justice requires a method that allows the principal investigator to explore it by approaching the question from multiple frames of reference. Through this approach, the principal investigator began to understand the phenomenology of the experience of remorse for this population. While the approach incorporates quantitative measures, it is, overall, a qualitative one. The empirical method is similar to triangulation but, for this study, is more appropriately labeled converging evidence. Support for this approach is similar to arguments that favor the individual case study approach. It strengthens the ability to bring to light the richness and variety of the individual's experience. According to Lukoff and Edwards, (2000), a hallmark of the case study approach is collection of data from many and varied sources. Gathering information from multiple sources lends itself well to the depth and multi-faceted view required for examining the complexity of an individual's experience of remorse. The principal investigator suggests that this argument also holds when investigating a construct such as remorse for a population. Further, use of multiple sources can reduce principal investigator bias and increase construct validity when the lines of evidence produce complementary or consistent results (Smith, 1988).

The study began with a description of the environment, Urban Peak Denver, a demographic analysis of the population, and a pilot study that included quantitative data from a paper-and-pencil test given to 32 participants, and focus groups. Because tools directly measuring remorse were not available, the principal investigator found it necessary to use tools that measure related constructs.

The principal investigator believed that a key strength of this study was its integration of different levels of information, thus giving depth and breadth to understanding the construct of remorse, specifically as experienced by the subject population. From a broader perspective, this study might be viewed as a step toward a more in-depth sociological case study of the remorse experience of this population.

Urban Peak Denver

Urban Peak Denver (UPD), a not-for-profit agency, serves approximately 700 homeless and runaway adolescents each year. UPD generally serves adolescents between ages 15 and 21. Some youth 21 and older are served in subsidized housing programs. Most youth under age 16 are referred back into social services. If youth under age 18 can be reunited with their families, UPD works toward this end. Otherwise, services cover such needs as overnight shelter, meals, case management, general advocacy (e.g. support with handling warrants and navigating social service or Medicaid systems), mental health counseling, medical services, GED classes, employment and education counseling, and subsidized housing. UPD has operated for over 16 years and was one of only two licensed homeless youth shelters in Colorado at the time of this study.

Supporters of UPD suggest a key strength is that young people are there because they choose to be. Youth staying at UPD must be motivated to work a case plan[8] geared toward helping them exit street life. UPD's operating philosophy uses a strengths-based, youth development approach. This means case plans begin where youth are in their lives and work

---

[8] Case plans include goals for youth to improve their situation. Staff members worked collaboratively with clients to create a plan that supported them in exiting the streets through goals that are reasonable for them based on their current mental and physical situation.

to use strengths, as identified collaboratively by case managers and youth, to create goals. Some youth have goals as basic as attending to hygiene or as challenging as staying alcohol-free or drug-free. While accessing services at UPD, youth must actively work on their case plan if they want to stay at the shelter for any prolonged period. Those who stay have accepted this requirement, even though they most likely have skills to survive, at least for the short-term, on the streets. Many lose services for a time if they do not work on goals or if they engage in extremely threatening or violent behaviors.

Demographic Description of the Population

The following operational definitions clarify parameters examined in this study.

Psychosocial issues – This rubric includes physical abuse or neglect, sexual abuse, a mental health diagnosis, and substance abuse. These determinations come from self-report, observation, or diagnosis by a clinician.

Involvement with social services – Youth with an open case through social services generally had issues in their family that resulted in removal of the youth from the home or some other intervention by social services. The relationship with social services usually ended when the youth reached age 18.

Active support from one or more family members – This indicated whether or not the case notes evidenced that the youth could seek out and receive support from a family member, or if a family member visited or engaged in conversation with the case manager in the interest of the youth. Family included parents (foster, adoptive, and biological), grandparents, aunts, uncles, sisters, and brothers.

Involvement with the criminal justice system – This indicated outstanding warrants or legal involvement (except traffic violations) for which youth might be fined or arrested.

Ethnicity – The database categorizes youth into six groups: White/Caucasian, Black, Hispanic, Asian/Pacific Islander, American Indian/Alaskan Indian, and Multi-Ethnic.[9]

Gender – In this study, it included male, female, and transgendered. Transgendered youth believe they were born into a body of the wrong sex. Their sexual orientation might be any of one of those listed below.

Sexual orientation – Sexual orientation, as indicated by youth, was broken down into heterosexual, homosexual, bisexual, and questioning.[10]

Data for this study was gathered from May 2001 through April 2002. Of the 503 youth in this study, 310 were males, 188 were females, and five were transgendered. Mean age was 19.2, median age was 19.8, and most common age is 20. Standard deviation from the mean was 1.76 years. Males were slightly older with a mean age of 19.3 years. Mean age for females was just under19 years old. Table 1 shows mean and median ages of the youth in relationship to psychosocial issues, involvement with social services, involvement in the criminal justice system, and active support from one or more family members. With exceptions of involvement with social services and active support from one or more family members, mean ages for youth with positive responses to these factors were slightly higher than for the entire population. The slightly younger age for involvement with social services reflected that youth age out of social services at 18, thus lowering average age. Regarding the slightly lower age for family support, it was possible that families, and youth themselves, tended to see older youth as less needy or less deserving of this support.

---

[9] For purposes of this study, multi-ethnic also refers to bi-ethnic.
[10] The label of questioning indicates youth who are uncertain of their sexual preference at some point during their stay in the shelter. Sometimes youth are labeled, for example, as heterosexual and later may demonstrate homosexual tendencies or engage in same sex prostitution. This may result in a label of questioning sexual orientation.

Table 1.

Mean, standard deviation from mean, and median ages for psychosocial factors

	Mean Age in years Total/Male/Female	Standard Deviation from Mean Total/Male/Female	Median Age in years Total/Male/Female
Physical Abuse	19.4/19.6/19.0	1.77/1.75/1.72	19.9/20.0/19.3
Sexual Abuse	19.7/20.2/19.5	1.64/1.58/1.63	20.5/21.5/20.2
Mental Health	19.4/19.6/19.2	1.64/1.58/1.70	19.9/20.0/19.6
Substance Abuse	19.4/19.6/19.0	1.65/1.59/1.70	19.9/20.0/19.3
Social Services	18.9/19.0/18.8	1.80/1.75/1.87	19.5/19.2/19.6
Criminal Involvement	19.2/19.3/19.0	1.44/1.34/1.69	20.7/20.8/20.7
Family Support	19.0/19.2/18.8	1.49/1.42/1.59	19.2/19.0/19.2

Table 2 shows a breakdown of youth in each demographic category, by frequency and percentage of subpopulations. Males comprised almost two-thirds of the population, and over half of it was Caucasian. The largest age group was between 19 and 20 years old. Two years later, in March 2004, the breakdown of gender, ethnicity, and age had not changed greatly, but did show the female population had risen to 40% from 37%, the Hispanic population had risen to 15% from 12%, the African American population had fallen to 16% from 18%, and number of minors had fallen from 17% to 13%.

Table 2.

Breakdown by gender, ethnicity and age

Gender	188 female (37%)		310 male (62%)		5 transgendered (1%)		
Ethnicity	19 American Indian/Alaskan (4%)	5 Asian/ Pacific Islander (1%)	90 Black (18%)	266 Caucasian (53%)	60 Hispanic (12%)	63 Multi-Racial (12%)	
Age	14 to 15 years - 10 (2%)	16 years - 29 (6%)	17 years - 47 (9%)	18 years - 78 (16%)	19 years - 102 (20%)	20 years - 120 (24%)	21 years - 87 (17%)	22 to 27 years olds 30 (6%)

Figure 1 shows that youth were most commonly Caucasian males, followed by Caucasian females, Black males, and then Black females. While there were many more males than females, this figure indicated that ethnic distribution between males and females was similar, with only a slight difference in distribution of Hispanic and Multi-ethnic youth.

Figure 1. Breakdown of ethnicity by gender

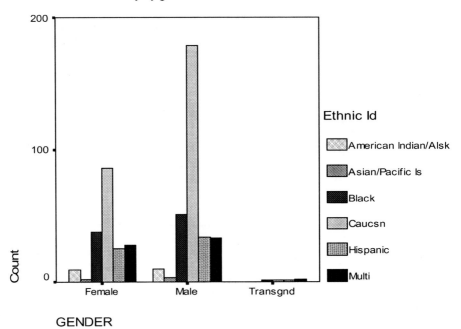

Figure 2. Breakdown of ethnicity by age

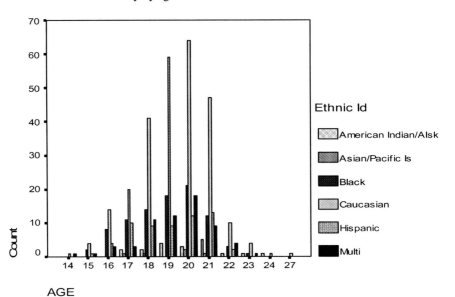

Figure 2. shows that age 20 was the most common age in each ethnic group, except

Hispanic and American Indian/Alaskan.

Table 3 describes the population by frequency and percentage of positive response for

the psychosocial issues, involvement with social services, involvement in the criminal justice

system, and active support from one or more family members. This is also broken down by

gender. The total population for each psychosocial issue was 503 youth, except where

indicated otherwise.

Table 3.

Psychosocial, criminal involvement and family support as function of gender

	Total	Female	Male	Transgendered
Physical Abuse	296 (59%)	131 (70%)	161 (52%)	4 (80%)
Sexual Abuse	114 (23%)	78 (41%)	33 (11%)	3 (60%)
Substance Abuse	356 (71%)	119 (63%)	233 (75%)	4 (80%)
Mental Health Diagnosis	321 (64%)	117 (62%)	200 (65%)	4 (80%)
Social Services	270 (54%)	105 (56%)	164 (53%)	1 (20%)
Criminal Involvement (385 youth)	218 (57%)	56 (40%)	162 (68%)	None reported
Family Support (379 youth)	280 (74%)	101 (69%)	177 (76%)	2 (40%)

The information in the table above shows females with a higher rate of reporting

physical abuse or neglect and sexual abuse, and of becoming involved social services than the

total population. Males had a higher rate of substance abuse, mental health diagnosis, criminal

involvement, and active support from one or more family members. Transgendered youth

showed high rates for physical abuse or neglect, sexual abuse, substance abuse, and mental

health diagnosis. While this was true for this population, due to the small number in this

group, it was unfounded to suggest these rates would hold true if the group were larger, or if

the participants were drawn from another population. Due to size of this group, it will be

excluded from the statistical analysis using chi-square.

Figure 3 shows a distribution of youth by number of psychosocial issues reported. Of

503 youth, 64 had all four psychosocial issues discussed in this study. The most common

number of psychosocial issues was two (152 youth). The second most common number of

psychosocial issues reported was three (136 youth). There were 119 youth with one reported

psychosocial issue and 32 without any of these issues reported.

Figure 3. Frequency of Psychosocial Issues

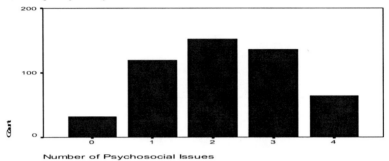

Figure 4 shows distribution of psychosocial issues by gender. While males clearly

peaked in the mid-range for psychosocial issues, female distribution was skewed toward the

high range of number of psychosocial issues.

Figure 4. Breakdown of number of psychosocial issues by gender

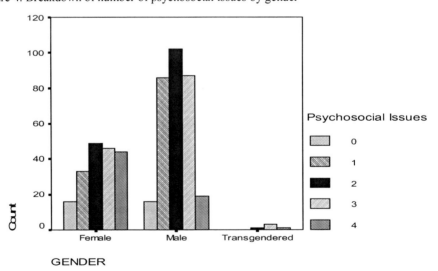

The following table gives the demographic breakdown of sexual orientation by gender.

Table 4. Breakdown of sexual orientation by gender

Sexual Orientation (340 youth)	Heterosexual	Bisexual	Homosexual	Questioning
	267 (79%)	44 (9%)	20 (6%)	8 (2%)
Females (137)	94 (69%)	33 (24%)	7 (5%)	3 (2%)
Males (199)	173 (87%)	9 (5%)	12 (6%)	5 (2%)
Transgendered (4)	1 (25%)	2 (50%)	1 (25%)	None Reported

Significant Correlations

This section discusses the significant correlations that emerged in the statistical analysis. It is formatted with a discussion followed by tables showing the factors being compared and the critical values for chi-square, based on degrees of freedom for each comparison. Dependent variable headers are listed across the top of the tables and independent variables are listed in the left-hand column.

Correlation of reporting of each psychosocial issue and gender, ethnicity, age, or involvement with social services – Table 5 shows the analysis of the relationship of physical abuse or neglect, sexual abuse, mental health diagnosis, and substance abuse, with gender, ethnicity, age, and involvement with social services.

Table 5. Correlation: Psychosocial/Gender, Ethnicity, Age, Social Services Involvement

	Gender	Ethnicity	Age	Social Services Involvement
Critical Value	3.841	11.070	14.067	3.841
Physical Abuse/Neglect	6.285	2.202	5.698	6.057
Sexual Abuse	49.950	8.838	15.556	7.735
Mental Health Diagnosis	0.128	4.388	10.623	2.349
Substance Abuse	2.330	3.692	5.446	0.172

There were significant correlations relating sexual abuse with gender, age, and involvement with social services. The correlation to gender was the strongest, and was a positive correlation between females and sexual abuse and a corresponding negative correlation between males and sexual abuse. There was a similar, though not as pronounced, correlation for females and males regarding physical abuse. Physical abuse and sexual abuse both correlated positively with the youth's involvement with social services, while substance abuse and mental health diagnosis did not. There was also a significant positive correlation between increasing age and reporting of sexual abuse. No significant correlations emerged between ethnicity and psychosocial issues.

Concerning sexual abuse and gender, it was not surprising that gender plays a role in this, particularly when the percentage of those reporting sexual abuse for the whole population was 23%, while that for females in this population compares at 41% and for males compares at 11%. It is important to note that potential for under-reporting, particularly by males, may have influenced this correlation. Positive correlation for females with physical abuse or neglect was also not surprising. This may not necessarily mean abuse or neglect was not occurring as much for males because, culturally, what may be viewed as physical abuse for females may not be viewed as such for males. Additionally, culturally, it was less likely that males would report abuse or be taken seriously if they did.

Positive significant correlation between reports of sexual abuse and physical abuse or neglect and involvement with social services also appears intuitively obvious. This was so because of required reporting laws and immediate involvement of social services, particularly regarding cases of reported sexual abuse of children.

Positive correlation of reports of sexual abuse with increasing age supports the proposition that youth may be reluctant to report the abuse until they are older and/or out of the home. Further exploration of this possibility would require knowing the age at which reported abuse took place and the age at which it was reported.

Correlation of involvement in the criminal justice system and reports of each psychosocial issue – There were two significant correlations found between psychosocial issues and involvement in the criminal justice system. The correlation between sexual abuse and involvement in the criminal justice system was an inverse relationship. Youth who reported sexual abuse had a higher expected frequency of also being involved with the criminal justice system than was actually reported. It was unclear at this point why this first significant correlation existed. On the other hand, there was a positive significant correlation between involvement in the criminal justice system and substance abuse. The second correlation corresponds well with the high rate of substance abuse in the total population (71%). One might reasonably expect a higher arrest and conviction rate for these youth because they were more likely to be caught for illegal possession of alcohol, possession of illegal drugs, or theft in order to purchase these substances.

Table 6.

Correlation: Criminal Justice System Involvement/Psychosocial Issues

	Physical Abuse/Neglect	Sexual Abuse	Mental Health Diagnosis	Substance Abuse
Critical Value	3.841	3.841	3.841	3.841
Criminal Justice System Involvement	0.0002	4.085	0.0015	4.452

Correlation of involvement in the criminal justice system and demographics, such as gender, ethnicity, and age – The analysis revealed a positive significant correlation between involvement in the criminal justice system and males.

Table 7.

Correlation: Criminal Justice/Gender, Ethnicity, Age

	Gender	Ethnicity	Age
Critical Value	3.841	11.070	14.067
Criminal Justice System Involvement	11.983	4.504	8.964

Correlation of active support from one or more family members and reports of each psychosocial issue – There was one significant correlation between active support from one or more family members and psychosocial issues. This was an inverse relationship with sexual

abuse. This means youth who had reported sexual abuse showed lower levels of family

support than expected based on statistical analysis. This was not particularly surprising.

Frequently in families when the balance of the family has been disturbed, even if it is a

balance based on dysfunction, the remainder of the family tends to rally together to restore the

balance to what it was. If an abused child reports it, he or she may be seen as the culprit who

has disturbed the balance. This child must either come back in line with the dysfunction, or be

rejected (Scarf, 1995). Rejoining the dysfunctional state is often out of the question in these

situations because forces outside the family (e.g. social services, a therapist, or law

enforcement officials) hinder the child from taking part in restoring the family to its previous

state. The child tends to be ostracized instead.

Table 8.

Correlation: Family Support/Psychosocial Issues

	Physical Abuse/Neglect	Sexual Abuse	Mental Health Diagnosis	Substance Abuse
Critical Value	3.841	3.841	3.841	3.841
Active Support from one or more family members	2.975	**6.337**	0.001	1.81E-05

Correlation of involvement in the criminal justice system and active support from one or more family members – Although this correlation did not demonstrate significance, it bears

importance to the purpose of this study. One might expect an inverse relationship between

involvement in the criminal justice system and active support from the family. A possible

explanation was that acting out with criminal behaviors was a plea for attention from the

family and it effectively brought them back in touch with the youth. Since the agency works

toward reunification, this advocacy for the youth with the family may have affected the

correlation, thus offsetting any tendency toward a negative correlation. More detailed data

might shed light on any relationships that may exist between these factors.

Table 9.

Correlation: Criminal Justice System Involvement/Family Support

	Active Support from one or more family members
Critical Value	3.841
Criminal Justice System Involvement	0.370

Correlation of total number of psychosocial issues reported and involvement with social services, involvement in the criminal justice system, and having active support from one or more family members – One significant correlation between involvement with social services and number of psychosocial issues reported was revealed. More reported psychosocial issues meant youth would more likely be involved with social services.

Table 10.

Correlation: Psychosocial Issues/Social Services, Criminal Justice, Family Support

	Social Services Involvement	Criminal Justice System Involvement	Active Family Support
Critical Value	9.488	9.488	9.488
# of Psychosocial Issues	**14.824**	0.891	1.522

Summary of the Demographic Analysis

In addition to the statistically significant correlations, there were useful descriptive statistics that allowed the principal investigator to make some generalizations for future exploration. This information demonstrates that, while the majority of the youth are heterosexual and Caucasian, there was diversity in ethnicity and sexual orientation. It shows that the majority are males, but that over one third of this population was female. Over half of both genders report physical abuse or neglect, have been involved with social services, have been involved with the criminal justice system, and have a mental health diagnosis, Slightly less than three-fourths have active support of some kind from one or more family members. Additionally, almost two-thirds of females and three-fourths of males have substance abuse issues.

While this database provided a good initial picture of these youth, the type of available data precludes other statistical tests that make further inferences possible, particularly regarding youth involvement in the criminal justice system. Significant correlations, such as the positive relationship between females and reported sexual abuse, seemed, for the most part, intuitively obvious. On the other hand, there were also correlations that may have seemed intuitively reasonable, such as an inverse relationship between involvement in the criminal justice system and support from one or more family members, and yet significance was not demonstrated in the data analysis.

The question might be whether the statistics are misleading, the data are misleading, or the intuitive reasoning was simply unfounded. It was also possible that the intuitive reasoning was well founded, but that the data collected was not specific enough. Perhaps also, had the data been parametric in nature, this might have changed the type of statistical tests suitable for use in this research. Examples of this include: if the data had provided the age at which youth became involved in social services and if the number of warrants or legal issues or the level of substance abuse could have been gathered. Had this been so, this statistical analysis might have yielded additional results.

The Pilot Study

Methods and Procedure

This study provided an opportunity to gain experience working with this population in a research format. It also was a trial use of the TOSCA-A[11] and focus group protocol. Thirty-two volunteers from the UPD population took the TOSCA-A. The guilt-proneness score on the TOSCA-A was used to determine participation in focus groups.

---

[11] With Dr. Tangney's approval, the principal investigator modified the wording in the instrument to increase applicability to life circumstances of the subject population.

TOSCA-A

The TOSCA-A measures the occurrence of guilt and shame proneness, as defined by

Tangney et al. (1991, 1992, & 2002), as well as other related constructs, including detachment

(indifference to circumstances), externalization (blaming of other or external circumstances),

alpha-pride (pride in self), and beta-pride (pride about one's actions). While the guilt-

proneness scale was of primary interest, other scales also provided data that was useful in

understanding the experience of remorse for this population. This tool which measures

constructs that are believed to be related to remorse was used because there was no other tool

available that measures remorse directly.

In studies of two different groups, one group of 372 college students and another

group of 269 late adolescents from an urban area with ethnic and socioeconomic diversity,

mean scores on the guilt scale were 57.47 (male)/60.05 (female) and 54.88 (male)/59.05

(female) respectively (Tangney et al., 2002). In two studies conducted by the author that will

be discussed in detail in subsequent sections, UPD youth's mean scores on the guilt scale

were 50.7/54.81 (male) and 55.5/61.79 (female). With one exception of master study females,

these studies suggested a possible downward trend in guilt-proneness that may correlate with

education level and/or socioeconomic status. If tendency toward guilt-proneness relates to

self-esteem, then, intuitively, it seemed to follow guilt scores would fall in moving from

college students to diverse urban youth to disadvantaged shelter youth.

Focus Groups

Focus groups are a useful tool; one that is intermediate to observation of groups in

their natural surroundings and individual open-ended interviews. They are particularly useful

for exploratory research. Marketing organizations frequently use them to help determine a direction for more quantitative research (Morgan, 1997). In this particular study, focus groups were useful because of their exploratory nature and also because remorse was an internal activity; focus group discussion had the potential to elicit information that provided an understanding of this internal process. Combined method studies, such as this one, according to Morgan (1997), are particularly useful because they contribute a uniquely multi-faceted perspective to understanding the phenomenon.

Important considerations in using this method included number of groups, size of the groups, selection of participants, composition of groups, focus of the protocol, and effective moderation. The rule of thumb for number of focus groups is three to five (Morgan, 1997). This provides enough information and yet is small enough to avoid saturation and redundancy of information gathered. This number is dependent upon the purpose of the study, existing knowledge of the topic, participants, and setting (Twohig & Putnam, 2002). While this phase of the study had three groups, the total number of focus groups for the entire project, including the subsequent master study, was seven. This number exceeds the maximum of the rule of thumb; however, again, due to the exploratory nature and limited information on the topic, the larger number of focus groups strengthens validity of the data gathered and did not result in redundancy.

In the pilot study, the limited number of eligible participants and availability of participants precluded having more than three groups. Regarding number of participants per group, Morgan suggests six to ten participants as a norm. The risk of smaller groups is they may not be able to sustain the discussion (Morgan, 1997). On the other hand, Gilbert and Gilbert (2003) suggested that smaller numbers may be more appropriate for certain groups and topics. Some populations, such as this study's population, may be more responsive in smaller groups. The principal investigator's experience with this population suggested that smaller groups would be more manageable and productive. If the groups had become too large, the result would have been some participants talking over each other and other participants having difficulty contributing their thoughts.

Since the facilitator was not directly involved in case plans it created a sense of neutrality and safety. The facilitator's familiarity with the population provided her with a level of skill in guiding discussions so they remained focused, but allowed for deviation to important topics as they arose. It also allowed the facilitator to handle, in an appreciative manner while maintaining flow of the discussion, the individual participant's need to express thought that was not directly on-task. Also important, was the facilitator's ability to take a focused, listening position, demonstrate intense curiosity, and effectively use nondirective, probing comments (Bullock & Jones, 1999). The facilitator's experience in training, facilitating, interviewing, and conducting investigations provided excellent training in skills necessary to conduct these focus groups. Additionally, as will be discussed in the data analysis section of the master study, it allowed the facilitator to know when the topic had become too sensitive for the group to continue an in-depth discussion.

Data Collection

Upon meeting with the volunteer participants, the principal investigator provided information about the study and asked them to sign the informed consent form (see Appendix A). They were told that they would be asked to complete a questionnaire at this meeting and may also be asked to participate in a focus group at a later date. Each volunteer was given an opportunity to read the informed consent form. The principal investigator also gave a brief verbal summary of the form and provided an opportunity for questions. This took approximately 20 minutes.

TOSCA-A. Before completion of the TOSCA-A, the topic of remorse was briefly explained and the instructions on the first page of the TOSCA-A were reviewed verbally by the principal investigator. The instrument required approximately 15 minutes to complete. Once participants finished the questionnaire, it was reviewed for completeness. An identifying number was written on it and was correlated to each participant's name. Soda and snacks were provided in appreciation of their time. As inducement, participants were also eligible for a Life Skills Class[12] credit in their case plan.

Focus Groups. The focus group protocol began with more structure to help guide the group toward the research topic. First, an introductory icebreaker question was asked, followed by a question that set the context by exploring the definition of restorative or reparative justice and showing the link between this and remorse. The two key questions for discussion were then introduced. To begin addressing these questions, participants were asked to list descriptors of behaviors or feelings they believed demonstrate remorse. Each person's voice was brought into the discussion by inviting them to share briefly, to the level of their comfort, a thought from their list. Morgan (1997) differentiates this question as a discussion-starter in contrast to the earlier icebreaker question. Focus groups were tape-recorded. Participants were served food during these meetings.

Recruitment and Selection

Participants were recruited through announcements to the community at weekly Community Breakfast and during other gathering times at the shelter. Announcements

---

[12] Clients at UPD were required to earn three Life Skills participation credits as part of their case plan. Only if the participant authorized the principal investigator to provide his or her name to her case manager, was this credit given.

included a request that participants be 18 to 21 years old. A further specification was that participants be able to read and comprehend English.

Those with a guilt-proneness score one-half standard deviation above the mean score for their gender were invited to participate in one of three focus groups conducted. Due to the large variation between individual scores and broad range of overall scores, using a full standard deviation would have resulted in too few focus group participants. This wide range and diversity of scores has been found to be common when conducting research with this population, and frequently requires adjustment in use of a standard deviation measure (C. Gilroy & J. Scandlyn, personal communication, January 12, 2004).

As indicated previously, the principal investigator believed that participants were more likely to share a personally meaningful story of remorse in the smaller groups. Morgan (1997) recommends that recruitment for focus groups should use a 20% rule of thumb for participant numbers. This means that, if four to five participants are sought, then five to seven participants should be recruited. In this case the principal investigator targeted approximately six youth each time and this resulted in three participants.

Considerable flexibility in scheduling the groups was necessary, as youth might be reluctant to participate during certain times of day, or have meetings, interviews or other commitments in their case plans, including engaging in a job search. This need for intensive coordination, along with the inclination of youth to sometimes agree to participate, when in reality they were reluctant, and then not show up was particularly challenging.

Instrument – TOSCA-A

This is a self-report tool containing 15 scenarios with four or five responses for which the respondent is asked to rate the likelihood of each response on a scale from 1 to 5, 1 being "not at all likely" and 5 being "very likely" (Tangney et al., 1991). The original TOSCA for

adults was modified to contain scenarios more relevant to adolescents aged 14 through 21.

The TOSCA-A test-retest reliability is .74 for the guilt scale. The Cronbach alpha measure of

internal consistency for the guilt scale ranges from .77 to .84. As indicated previously, the

TOSCA-A was further modified with minor verbiage changes more relevant to this

population.

Results for the Pilot Study

Data from the questionnaires was compiled and compared with data from a study of

urban youth by Tangney and Dearing (2002). Table 11 replicates data from the urban youth

study. Table 12 shows results for the 32 shelter youth.

Table 11.

Mean scores from Tangney and Dearing (2002, Appendix B, p. 237) study of ethnically and socioeconomically diverse urban youth aged 18 to 21 years [13]

Gender	Shame	Guilt	Externalization	Detachment	Alpha Pride	Beta Pride
Female	34.74	59.05	33.71	30.95	19.01	20.61
n=152	(8.38)	(6.65)	(6.51)	(5.10)	(2.57)	(2.33)
Male	32.94	54.88	35.25	32.38	18.75	19.81
n=117	(6.98)	(8.18)	(6.23)	(4.52)	(2.54)	(2.02)

Table 12.

Mean scores for pilot study - shelter population

Gender	Shame	Guilt	Externalization	Detachment	Alpha Pride	Beta Pride
Female	37.58	55.50	34.25	25.83	16.92	18.83
n=12	(9.83)	(8.53)	(7.16)	(6.81)	(2.97)	(2.25)
Male	35.60	50.70	36.20	29.05	16.05	17.05
n=20	(11.70)	(12.30)	(9.84)	(6.70)	(4.07)	(4.42)
Total	36.34	52.50	35.47	27.84	16.38	17.72
n=32	(10.91)	(11.14)	(8.86)	(6.82)	(3.67)	(3.81)

Based on selection criteria stated previously, focus group participants must have

minimum scores of 61 for females and 56 for males. Due to availability of participants, only 9

---

[13] Standard deviations appear in parenthesis below means. Shame, Guilt, and Externalization scores are derived from 15 items each, Detachment from 10 items, and Alpha and Beta Pride from five items each. Items are rated on a 5-point scale (1-5). Totals are not available in published work.

of the 14 who met these minimum scores participated in the focus groups. Five (36%) were

female and nine (64%) were male.

Scores for this population on the TOSCA-A differed from the urban youth studied by

Tangney and Dearing (2002) in that the shelter youth were comparatively higher in shame and

externalization and lower in guilt, detachment, alpha-pride, and beta pride. Interestingly,

while the scores did differ in these ways, there are numerous patterns that demonstrated some

consistencies in how the scores differed. The most notable pattern was that in both groups

females scored higher than males in moral emotions of guilt and shame and were more likely

to demonstrate both alpha and beta pride. Males were more likely than females in both groups

to demonstrate externalization and detachment. Figure 5 shows that where scores varied, they

varied in the same direction and by a similar number of percentage points for both males and

females.

Figure 5. Comparison of Urban and Shelter Populations

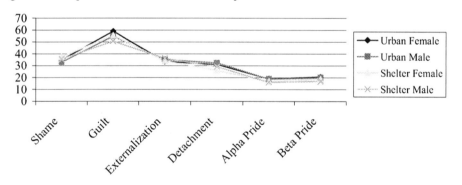

Discussion of the Pilot Study

Based on work by Tangney and Dearing (2002) and the challenges participants have

faced in their lives, it was not surprising that their TOSCA-A scores were lower for guilt and

higher for shame, in comparison to a group that was most likely composed of individuals who had experienced less trauma. With higher shame also comes higher need to externalize and lower alpha pride and beta pride. One might also expect these youth would be more likely to detach due to difficult life circumstances many have faced. Additionally, Tangney et al. (1992) found that guilt correlates negatively with detachment. Based on this, the prediction would be that lower guilt scores would correlate with higher detachment scores. As shown in Table 12 and Figure 5, however, this was not the case. The size of the group could potentially explain this, but with all the other patterns correlating with the urban youth study, it seems unlikely that size would have impacted this score only. It was more likely that something about the population accounted for this. One possibility was that the youth at UPD are learning to become more aware of their circumstances and histories and to re-engage their feelings. Staff members strive to create an environment where youth can begin to be more open and trusting and are expected to take responsibility for themselves and their actions. With that, these young people may become less detached.

Overall demographics of the nine focus group participants were similar to the demographics of the entire group regarding gender and age. Of the nine, 33% were female and 66% were male. Average age for males was 19 and for females was between 18 and 19. Ethnic breakdown was 78% Caucasian, 11% American Indian, and 11% Black. Gender mix for the individual focus groups, including the principal investigator was: 50% male and 50% female for group 1; 75% male and 25% female for group 2; and 25% male and 75% female for group 3. As will be discussed further in limitations and delimitations, this aspect of group composition had a noticeable effect during focus group discussions.

The three focus group discussions each touched on many similar themes relating to remorse. When contemplating what the experience of remorse might be for them, they took into consideration severity of harm, intentionality on their part, and their ability to relate to the person they had harmed. They also spoke of their life histories and experiences that blocked them from accessing emotions such as remorse. Additionally, participants in different groups talked about mental, emotional, physical, and transformational aspects of remorse as they experienced it.

Many concepts they discussed about how remorse would feel for them were the same as what they would look for in someone else to determine whether or not that person was truly remorseful. Other indications they would look for were signs of sincerity, direct eye contact, and a "vibe" that tells them that the person was truly sorry. They would also look for a notable change in behavior.

While many themes were the same between groups, there was striking difference in the stress that each group placed on various aspects of remorse. The first group seemed more focused on emotional and visceral experience of remorse. They spoke of the deep sorrow of remorse and physical experience of it in their bodies. They placed importance on direct eye contact and a heartfelt apology in determining remorse. The second group was more intellectual, as their analysis led to formulating a framework for remorse expressed by the three factors of relationship, severity of the harm, and intentionality. Whether or not and how much remorse was experienced was dependent upon these three factors. The third group made many comments about remorse as transformation. In this case, somehow a reality check occurs and the person feels deeply remorseful, which results in a life transformation. A truly remorseful person must rehabilitate the self as reparation for the harm and give back to society in other ways as well.

Based on focus group discussion, this population has a strong sense of behaviors that demonstrate remorse and how they would experience it. Several of them indicated existence of factors that inhibit their ability to experience remorse. Most notable among these was desensitization due to drug abuse and due to abuse or neglect they suffered. This might suggest that they would be more detached in their questionnaire responses. Interestingly, the male mean score on detachment was three points lower for focus group participants than for the larger group of male questionnaire participants. The female mean detachment score was almost six points lower than that of the larger group of female participants. It seems to present a paradox that these young people stated that they did not feel enough and were desensitized to harm they may have caused, when the very awareness that they might want to feel more about it suggested the opposite. This phenomenon may relate to comments the group made concerning remorse, specifically that someone who feels remorse feels powerless to fix the problem, that there was not enough they can do to make amends. Perhaps they also sensed that their level of feeling and taking responsibility was not appropriately proportionate to harm they may have caused or to harm caused to them. This possibility offers a possibility for further investigation. Another related question arose regarding their harsh judgment of themselves (or, in some cases, of their parents who may have harmed them) for re-offending, even if they felt remorse for their actions. Some comments in the focus group indicated the youth view re-offending as a lack of remorse.

All groups saw the importance of feeling some human connection to the individual they harmed in order to experience remorse, even if it was just to see the individual humanity of the person. This shows some correlation with Shaw's (1989) discussion regarding importance of relatedness, and that realization that one has committed a transgression against self or other requires a sense of relatedness. One participant commented that when he harmed someone, it was as if neither he nor the other person were truly present. Remorse can only come when the person doing the harm can see the humanity of each person.

Two of three groups spoke about justification for doing harm. If it was justified in the mind of the person doing the harm, then it was less likely to result in remorse. Likewise, for all three groups, if harm was done deliberately, they were less likely to see the perpetrator as remorseful. All three groups also maintained that severity of harm was important to the likelihood of a remorse experience. It was the second group's discussion, as previously mentioned, that elucidated the possibility of a 3-dimensional model. One axis would have increasing severity, the second would have increasing relationship to the person harmed, and the third would be decreasing intentionality. As these factors moved in the stated directions, remorse was a more likely result. While this model was an oversimplification, it does offer some understanding of how these three factors might interact dynamically with regard to remorse for this population.

The groups said that remorse was also a physical experience. It can bring a sense that one was dragging one's body through the motions of life. It can be seen in the eyes. It is, as previously stated, a "vibe" that one picks up from people when they are truly remorseful. It was literally felt in one's body, specifically one's heart. The first group was the one most willing to explore this aspect of remorse. Every member of this group could articulate how they experienced remorse physically. One member in particular was able to articulate what to look for in someone else, while, unknowingly, simultaneously demonstrating it. The other two groups attempted to express the physical sense of remorse, but neither group discussed it as long or as clearly as the first group.

In a society that reinforces intellect as the principal way of knowing and understanding experiences, it was surprising that even one of the groups could be so articulate about the physical experience of remorse. Connecting with the physical sense of this experience offered valuable potential for increasing understanding. It may be a path to owning and internalizing into conscious awareness such experiences as remorse. Westen (1998) has done considerable work showing that unconscious affect and attitudes impact physiology as much as, and maybe more than, conscious affect and attitude. Therefore, it may follow that becoming aware of physiological experiences will re-connect awareness to this unconscious affect and attitude. Further exploration of the physical aspect of remorse may provide insight into understanding the remorseful experience for this population.

As mentioned previously, the most convincing evidence of remorse for these participants was changed behavior, a life change, or some kind of transformation. Members of the third group suggested that this was the best way to apologize. The third group in particular felt strongly that the phrase "I'm sorry" was overused. Saying this was a way to "shut people up" and to avoid feeling badly about what one has done. Moore (1989) specifically addressed this phenomenon, calling it false remorse. He also suggested that it was a method to avoid the pain of remorse. He called it a "diversionary substitute for true remorse . . . [and] the superficial expression of repentance" (Moore, 1989, p. 88). While the value of and approach to an apology was expressed differently in each group, all three mentioned that a substantial life change was what best demonstrated true remorse – – even if that change was to better one's own circumstances and thereby become a valued contributor to society (one of the goals of restorative justice).

In light of this, it was important to remember why these young people are at UPD. Even a reticent participant in the third group stated that he was at UPD to try to change. Though he claimed skepticism about his ability to change, he was still working on his case plan. Additionally, the young people in the shelter saw others who were in different phases of the program. They had opportunities to see young people who had been through the program and were on their way to becoming self-sufficient young adults. These young people were in the process of transformation, so it was not surprising that they expected those who are remorseful to act out that remorse in a very real way by changing their lives.

These young people's thoughts about the transformative power of remorse echo a description of remorse by Stern (1989):

> Remorse matures experience, and as such, hallows the sacredness of contrition and restitution. What results is an atonement with that which is of central worth to a person's existence. Remorse peaks beyond its foundations, making meaningful use of both guilt and regret. (Stern, 1989, p. 2)

What these young people talked about stands in contrast to Greenberg and Fitzpatrick's (1989) and Hauck's (1989) descriptions of remorse that characterize it as a painful, unproductive emotion that focuses on personal inadequacy. This description was not what these participants were relating in the focus groups. There was pain and unrest, but they spoke more about how this experience moves someone to make changes. In terms of Tangney et al.'s work (1992, 2002), what these authors are alluding to ties more closely to Tangney's description of shame, or guilt interlaced with shame.

While these young people clearly articulated their construct of remorse, there are comments suggesting that they have not completely internalized this moral response. It was striking that they spoke eloquently about remorse and how important transformation was in demonstrating true remorse, and yet, made comments that were unforgiving of people who show remorse and then repeat the behavior. This suggests that they understood remorse and believed in its transformative power. Yet, they were aware that they could fall back. Indeed many of these young people have cycled back through harmful behaviors several times, but hopefully it was a shorter cycle and they recovered more readily. The recrimination with which these young people view this cycling back is similar to Kierkegaard's (1844/1980) view that "the new sin is the most terrible punishment for sin" (p. 173). He suggested that the sinner who "shudders at the thought of his sin" (p. 173) becomes distraught at the thought of having re-offended, not realizing that the repeat offense is its own punishment.

Remorse can have remarkable and immediate transformative power, but most often, it was probably slower transformation than these young people wanted, as they internalize it increasingly through their experiences. When asked if the source of their anguish for having done harm was internal or external, responses were mixed. Some participants expressed higher extrinsic motivation, while others indicated higher intrinsic motivation. Based on these discussions, the investigator believes that the youth are, essentially, in the early stages of a process of internalization and discovery of their own sense of values to guide their actions. Even more importantly, in May's (1983) terms, they are in the process of becoming. Taking this thought further, perhaps they are reaching toward their potential and suffering from ontological guilt in the mode of *Eigenwelt*, or a sense of forfeited potentiality (May, 1983).

CHAPTER 4. THE MASTER STUDY

Encouraged by the results of the preliminary study, the principal investigator chose to conduct a larger, more in-depth study which included an additional parameter for choosing focus groups and conduct of individual case studies. The TOSCA-A and focus groups were administered and conducted in the same manner as the pilot study.

Methods and Procedure

The TOSCA-A was administered to 45 volunteers from the population, followed by the conduct of four focus groups. Based on scores on the guilt scale of the TOSCA-A, focus group participants were divided into groups of high guilt-proneness and low guilt-proneness. In the next step, four single clinical case studies, one extracted from each focus group, were selected for closer, in-depth examination. Individual clinical case study participants were selected based on revelation of a personally meaningful remorse experience during focus group discussion. Individual clinical case studies included administration of the Harder and Zalma (1990) Personal Feelings Questionnaire - - 2 (PFQ - - 2), administration of Murray's Thematic Apperception Test (Morgan & Murray, 1935), and review of case notes and case history from the Agency database.

Focus Groups

In the current study, using both high and low guilt-proneness scores increased the number of eligible participants. The principal investigator hoped to increase number of participants in each group from three to four in order to capture a broader spectrum of perspectives in the population. The transient nature of the population and level of dependability, however, rendered this goal unattainable. For that reason, each of the four focus groups had three participants. While this did not help to provide more varied input from a higher number of participants, it did continue to allow groups to be manageable, considering needs of the population. Even with three participants, it was challenging at times to assure that each voice was heard. The principal investigator, as facilitator, often found it necessary to use her facilitation skills to balance input from each participant.

On the other hand, a difference between the pilot study and this later study may have affected the outcome of the focus group portion. The facilitator no longer had an office located at the shelter. This reduced the level of day-to-day visual contact and, therefore, familiarity between the facilitator and youth. This may have undermined, to some degree, comfort level with the facilitator.

Individual Case Studies

It was important to note that participants for this step were already pre-selected by guilt-proneness scores - - either high or low. This provided further understanding of the comparison between these two groups. The limiting factor of the case study method most frequently identified is that depth and breadth for one case, or in this instance, four cases, is gained at the expense of generalizability of the findings to other cases and situations. The combination of this method with larger scale quantitative and qualitative analysis, however, broadens and deepens the scope of understanding this study provides. Using statistics from the database in individual case studies also brought the lens back around to help provide another level of understanding of findings of the large-scale statistical analysis of the database. Greene, Caracelli, and Graham (1989) offer additional reasons for combining multiple methods. These reasons include: overlapping and different facets of the same phenomenon may emerge; if used sequentially, the first method may inform the second method; conflicting and fresh perspectives may emerge; and adding scope and breadth. In this particular study, all of these reasons are applicable.

The TAT was used in individual case studies to elicit unconscious expression of remorse and other related experiences. The projective hypothesis proposes that when individuals attempt to understand vague or ambiguous stimuli they interpret them such that it reveals their own needs, feelings, experiences, patterns of being in the world, and cognitive style (Kaplan & Saccuzzo, 1997). This suggests that the TAT offered possibility of plumbing the depths of the experience of remorse for these individuals. While the case study approach does not necessarily provide data that can be generalized to the population, the fact that this was nested within a study of broader scale allowed some correlations to be made with focus group and TOSCA-A results. Conducting four case studies offered the opportunity to look for discernable patterns between individuals.

Data Collection

The same process was followed as for the pilot study, with the exception that participants were also told of the possibility of participating in an individual case study.[14]

TOSCA-A

During administration, as in the pilot study, snacks were again served, and participants were offered the option of a Life Skills Credit.

Focus Groups

As in the pilot study, meetings were tape-recorded and food was served.

---

[14] Storage of data will be as follows: Informed consent forms are kept separate from data in a locked box and will be destroyed after three years. Data collected in raw and transcribed forms is kept anonymous, stored in a locked container accessible only to the principal investigator and will also be destroyed after three years. Transcribed data in the form of computer disks containing anonymous spreadsheets and anonymous response listings from all participants to each question will be kept indefinitely for future research. In the event of sudden death of the principal investigator, materials will be forwarded to the committee chair of this project for appropriate and confidential handling or destruction.

Individual Case Studies

The final piece, the four individual case studies, included an in-depth study of each selected participant's case history, notes, and demographics recorded in the client database, administration of the PFQ - - 2 (Harder & Zalma, 1990), and Morgan and Murray's Thematic Apperception Test (TAT).

The PFQ - - 2 provided further information regarding the possible relationship remorse may have to shame and guilt. The participants were given verbal instructions for filling out the questionnaire before completion. Since this piece only required 5-10 minutes, it was administered just prior to administration of the TAT.

For administration of the TAT, the intent was to select cards that would elicit the themes previously named (i.e., empathy, remorse, guilt, and shame) and to pull for themes of parent/child relationships, blaming, anger, and desire to make reparation. The latter themes are important due to believed correlations between them and empathy, remorse, guilt, and shame. The principal investigator chose a set of cards most likely to draw out these themes. This set included cards 1, 3BM, 3GF, 4, 5, 6BM, 6GF, 7BM, 7GF, 8BM, 13B, 14, 15, 17GF, 18BM, 18GF, and 20. Selection of these cards was based on descriptions of the pictures themselves, as well as Bellak's (1971) descriptions of the kind of information these cards tend to yield, such as guilt, shame, remorse, and parental relationships. The principle investigator administered the TAT in consultation with a Licensed Psychologist in the State of Colorado who has experience with this tool.

Setting the context for drawing the desired themes required some introduction of the general topic of the research, along with a modification of the general TAT instructions. This required careful selection of words so that the framework was set without actually leading the participant and thus, inadvertently, shaping the stories in such a way that he or she believed the right answer was to incorporate a particular theme such as remorse. The interview began with an introduction including remarks of confidentiality and anonymity. The following script was used: *The purpose of my research is to learn how different people may respond in a variety of situations where they have, whether deliberate or not, caused some type of harm to someone or something. I am going to show you a set of pictures chosen specifically for this purpose so that you can tell me a story about how you think the people might be responding. Include in your story what happened just before the scene in the picture, what is happening currently, and the outcome. Be as creative as you like.*

After each administration, the primary investigator and participant spent a few minutes debriefing and covering any questions the participant had. Discussion of progress of the youth in his or her case plan often was a topic during this time as well. The principal investigator then thanked the youth for his or her time and contribution and gave the youth a $25 gift packet for the movie theater.

Recruitment and Selection

Again, unlike the pilot study, this phase included four focus groups that incorporated not only groups with participants who had high guilt-proneness scores, but also those with participants who had low guilt-proneness scores. This division of focus group participants offered potential to understand the relationship of the TOSCA-A guilt scale with ability to experience remorse, or to experience it in a certain way.

Participants whose guilt scores were a minimum of one half of a standard deviation above and below the mean score for their gender were invited to take part in focus groups. Eliciting participation seemed far more challenging in this later study than it did in the pilot study, perhaps due to the change in office space that had occurred for the principal investigator and the resulting decreased familiarity of the youth with her.

One case study participant was selected from each focus group. In addition to the participant having shared a personally meaningful experience of remorse in the focus group, selection also depended upon availability and willingness of the participant. In two instances, one for the high guilt-proneness group and one for the low guilt-proneness group, the first choices of case study participants were unavailable and second choices were used instead. An example of a personally meaningful story was one that was told in the pilot study. This youth told a story of a time when she was completely enraged and unable to think of anything except escape from the situation in which she found herself. Her attempt to escape resulted in knocking someone down and causing a lifelong impairment to this individual. She spoke of the depth of her regret for this and her subsequent efforts to make major changes in her life. She saw this as a pivotal incident in transforming her life. Another example from this later study was a youth who told a story of having lost all of his services at UPD due to involvement with drug distribution. He endured considerable hardship without those services and had to work very hard to restore the damaged trust of UPD staff in order to regain them.

Instruments

TOSCA-A

The modified TOSCA-A used in the pilot study was also used in this study.

Personal Feelings Questionnaire - - 2

Another scale offering further information about guilt-proneness and shame-proneness is the PFQ - - 2 (Harder & Zalma, 1990). The PFQ - - 2 is a self-report assessment of 22 questions, ten relating to shame and six relating to guilt. This assessment asks participants to rate the frequency with which they experience each of the feelings from 0 (not at all) to 4 (almost continuously or continuously). Scale coefficients alpha (N=63) are .78 and .72 for shame and guilt, respectively (Harder & Zalma, 1990). Scale test-retest reliability coefficients over a two-week period (N=27) are .91 and .85 for shame and guilt, respectively (Harder & Zalma, 1990). Appendix C provides a reproduction of the questionnaire.

There are conflicting opinions about what the PFQ - - 2 measures. Tangney and Dearing (2002) maintain that this scale more closely captures shame because it asks participants to assess the degree of negative feelings they have, thereby resulting in a negative self-judgment. This is in contrast to the TOSCA-A, which asks participants to identify how they might respond in a given situation. The response is then categorized with the assessment tool as having implicit guilt or shame feelings. In the TOSCA-A there is no requirement for self-judgment on the part of the participant. Ferguson and Stegge (1998) suggest, however, that guilt and shame are not as different as is suggested by TOSCA results and that the PFQ - - 2 measures both guilt and shame. Further, that high proneness to either can result in a tendency toward psychopathology. They also propose that the TOSCA-A's guilt scale not only captures guilt in the relevant scenarios, but also captures a measure of self-adjustment, which would naturally correlate less well with psychopathology. In any event, this study seeks to understand the remorse experience, whether its characteristics are self-adjusting, self-actualizing, or self-destructive. Therefore, both tools were used in this exploration.

Thematic Apperception Test

The TAT is a set of 30 pictures of ambiguous situations, primarily social, and one blank card. The test was originally designed for the use of 20 of the cards, by choosing only

82

one of two that are indicated for boy/male or girl/female or boy. The standard approach to

administering the test is to ask the participant to make up a story that incorporates the image

he or she is about to be shown. The story should include: what is happening in the picture;

what happened just prior to the scene depicted; how people in the picture are feeling; what

they are thinking; and the outcome (Teglasi, 2002). The participant may be further

encouraged to indulge his or her literary imagination.

    While the TAT receives considerable criticism due to its believed psychometric

failings, it is a valuable tool for gaining access to unconscious material that allows the

investigator potentially to gain a deeper understanding of the phenomenology of the

participant's experience (Taylor, personal communication, January 27, 2003). A reasonable

query is whether or not we are subjecting this test to standards that are not applicable to what

it accomplishes. According to Rosenzweig (1999), who states that he collaborated very

closely with Morgan, this test was originally used like a structured interview that heavily

depended upon intuition and expertise of the examiner. Later, Murray, along with Leopold

Bellak (Abrams, 1999), proposed a needs-press scheme for scoring. To date, there are

numerous methods of scoring responses. In the needs-press approach, need is what the hero of

the story needs and press is the force in the external environment to which that need is

exposed. For example, if the hero is in love with a woman and the woman in turn despises

him, then love is the need and hate is the press. According to Bellak (1971), this system is not

widely used because, in addition to difficulty in mastering the need concept, it can take four

or five hours to interpret 20 cards. Bellak developed a form that he originally called the Bellak

TAT short form (Abrams, 1999). This form had ten categories including: Main theme; Main

hero; Main needs and drives of hero; Conception of the environment (world); Parental, contemporary, and junior figures (interpersonal object relations); Significant conflicts; Nature of anxieties; Main defenses against conflicts and fears; Adequacy of the superego as manifested by 'punishment' for 'crime'; and Integration of the ego (Bellak, 1971). The layout for this form was a columnar listing of these ten categories, followed by a column for the story created about each card and a summary column. There was also an optional checklist for ego function and adaptive regression in the service of the ego. This spreadsheet format makes it relatively easy for the administrator to see emerging themes and patterns across the series of stories. Bellak's approach has been the most widely used for six decades (Schneidman, 1999).

Schneidman (1999) further suggests that of the many other approaches to scoring, the majority can be categorized into five groups. These five groups are normative, hero oriented, intuitive, interpersonal, and perceptual. He proposes that analysts can prefer one of these as primary, and use another secondarily, and that, with the TAT, all most likely use the intuitive approach, at least secondarily. Interestingly, Schneidman (1999) has listed Bellak in four of the five categories. As one might expect, the normative grouping is the most quantitative and structured approach, and the intuitive is viewed as the least structured. McClelland (1999) has suggested still another scoring approach that is clearly quantitative. While strongly in favor of this approach, he openly acknowledges that it runs contrary to Murray's belief in capturing the whole of the person, rather than breaking the individual down into quantifiable parts (McClelland, 1999).

Data Analysis

TOSCA-A

As in the pilot study, TOSCA-A results were scored using the key provided by Tangney and Dearing (2002). Mean scores were determined for each parameter of the

TOSCA-A for the group as a whole and for males and females separately. The standard deviation was determined separately for male and female guilt-proneness scores. One half of the standard deviation above and below the mean for guilt-proneness scores for males and females was used to determine participation in high and low guilt-proneness scores.

Focus Groups

As previously noted, the focus groups were taped. Any body language observed was noted in writing during the group meetings. The notes and tapes for each focus group were reviewed after each group. Themes were noted and compared with themes from pilot study focus groups. This is a standard practice with focus groups so that the investigator can look for themes that require further clarification, questions that are not eliciting desired feedback, or areas that are not fully covered (Krueger & Casey, 2000). Once all focus groups were completed the principal investigator again listened to each focus group tape for themes and then listened to transcribe each tape. The identified themes were each numbered. The transcriptions were reviewed and the comments were numbered according to the theme heading under which they fit most closely. The pattern of themes was then examined for which themes appeared both in low and high guilt-proneness groups and those that were exclusive to one or the other. Themes that were unique to individual groups were also noted.

As in the pilot study, the nature of these groups was largely exploratory. In this phase, however, having information from prior focus groups offered an opportunity to look for and code themes that repeated, or did not repeat. Previous themes included remorse as a physical experience, importance of relatedness, life changes and transformation that occur due to remorse, intentionality in commission of harm, and importance of severity of that harm. While repeated themes were observed, it was still necessary to be aware of any new themes that arose. In this phase of the study, there was opportunity to look for differences between high and low guilt-proneness groups. It also provided an opportunity to observe when the groups did not necessarily differ. Specific themes from this study are discussed in the results section that follows.

Morgan (1997) points out that in focus groups there is some conflict about the unit of analysis, many suggesting that it is the group itself. Morgan, to the contrary, suggests there is interplay between the individual and the group and, therefore, both are units of analysis. In the pilot study focus groups, the principal investigator observed this dynamic. This makes composition of the groups very important, not only from the perspective of individual personalities, but also, most notably, gender balance. Groups in which the gender balance was skewed to one side or the other seemed to have a different tone. For example, in the pilot study, when there were three females (including the principal investigator, as facilitator) and one male, the male was clearly more subdued than the females in that group and than any males in the other groups. A second example also occurred in the pilot study when the participants were all males with whom the facilitator had a rapport outside of the group. There was an undercurrent of competition for the facilitator's attention. These dynamics and others continued as important factors in this subsequent study in collection and analysis of data. How and if these dynamics were influential is included in the individual focus group discussion of the results section.

In addition to examining focus group feedback, the principal investigator also used a two-tailed t-test to identify any significant differences between the TOSCA-A mean scores of the low guilt-proneness focus group participants and the high guilt-proneness focus group participants. This was done at a level of .05 significance. This was done for both the pilot study and master study focus group participants. Details of this analysis are in the Results section beginning with Table 20 and ending with Table 23.

Individual Case Studies

The principal investigator listened to each tape of the TAT three times, recording notes on a copy of the TAT Score Spreadsheet shown in Appendix D. The PFQ - - 2 guilt and shame scores were determined by averaging the responses. Each case study participant's case notes were reviewed and a historical outline was created from their case note history. As each results section was written, the principal investigator again reviewed the TAT spreadsheet and provided a subjective phenomenological analysis that combined the participant's history, demographics, and stories told and highlighted the parts of this analysis that revealed aspects of the individual's remorse experience.

Limitations and Delimitations

An overarching delimitation of this study was its focus on the experience of remorse for a very specific population; namely, youth who were homeless or runaway, or both. They had faced very adverse circumstances in their lives and were working to do something about their life situations. While this study provided information about this population, it may not be generalizable to a larger youth population that has not faced this level of adversity. It also may not pertain to youth in similar circumstances who have not taken initiative to work to change their circumstances.

Self-selection was an important consideration. While for the pilot study, demographics of participants closely reflected demographics of the larger client population, those of youth in this study did not match as closely with the larger population. It was also possible, in both studies, that willingness to participate differentiated them from the general shelter population.

Further, due to small numbers of participants in focus groups, demographics of this group did not fully match the larger population. Participants in both steps may, generally, be more participatory and also be more emotionally and psychologically open to exposing themselves to the process. This may be balanced, on the other hand, by a bias that clients who were highly motivated to find employment and further their education were less available to participate.

A limitation of the questionnaire was difficulty of accommodating young people with limited reading ability. While in the pilot study, one participant was accommodated in this factor by the principal investigator reading the questions and answers to him, it was time consuming and could not be done readily for a large number of young people. It was also possible that, unknown to the principal investigator, level of reading comprehension for other participants may have impacted their understanding of the questions. Efforts to be sensitive to this through previous information about participants and observation of them as they completed the questionnaire should have mitigated this. In both the pilot study and the master study, the fact that overall scores resulted in similar patterns as the Tangney and Dearing (2002) study suggests that this was the case.

Another possible limitation of the questionnaire was that, while items on it appear not to present a threat to self-esteem when answered honestly, there was some potential for participants to engage in impression management and answer as they thought they should answer in order to be perceived positively. Additionally, if participants had a personality disorder, whether or not it was diagnosed, this might influence answers. For example, a youth with a diagnosed condition who has chosen not to take medication that day or one who has not been diagnosed may respond from a place of paranoia. It was also possible that a participant could deliberately choose to answer in a contrary fashion. The principal investigator believed that the former was a more likely occurrence than the latter. These youth have acquired survival skills that do include impression management and, in this environment, that activity was more likely to be one of endearing themselves rather than alienating others. To mitigate this concern, instructions from the questionnaire that clearly stated there was no right or wrong answer were verbally restated for participants before completion. Further, the principal investigator, not being a member of program staff, was less likely to be viewed as influential in participants's program services. There was less emotional and psychological connection than with program staff. Therefore, it was unlikely participants would perceive a threat to connections that were important to them. In the latter case of deliberate misrepresentation, use of data gathered from multiple levels and by various means helped mitigate this possibility.

The focus group protocol (see Appendix B) worked well in the pilot study and there was no need for procedural changes. The limitation with focus groups was the small number of participants. Interestingly, make-up of this group generally reflected ethnic and gender diversity of the larger group of participants. While it did not completely match percentages of the questionnaire group due to the small number of focus group participants, there was diversity in the total population of these participants.

Due to the small size of individual focus groups, this diversity did not carry over into the composition of these individual groups. There were noticeable dynamics, regarding gender imbalances and personality mix that arose as an undercurrent during discussions. The facilitator was sensitive to these dynamics and guided the discussion to adjust for these dynamics. The impact of these dynamics seemed to lessen in the master study. While the smaller groups were helpful in working with this particular population, raising the number of participants in each group from three to five would have been helpful in generating more discussion and more diversity in discussion. The skills of the facilitator could have mediated this so that an increase would most likely not result in disruption of the group or in stifling participation for those who are not comfortable participating in large groups. It would also lessen the potential impact of gender imbalance and likelihood of dominance of the group by one particular personality. Unfortunately, the nature of the population and the relocation of the principal investigator to an offsite office made it extremely difficult to coordinate schedules of participants with the investigator and the number of participants did not increase.

Availability of youth was another limitation. The transient nature of the population made it challenging to have youth available for follow-up steps, such as occurred with focus groups. This was also true for individual case studies, although the principal investigator was able to adjust for this and engage suitable replacements.

CHAPTER 5. RESULTS

TOSCA-A

Table 13 shows mean scores for this study's population. Demographic make-up of these 45 participants was 14 (31%) females and 31 (69%) males. The average age was just under 19. The ethnic breakdown was 47% Caucasian, 20% Black, 16% Hispanic, 13% Multi-ethnic, 2% American Indian, and 2% Asian/Pacific Islander.

Table 13.

Mean scores from the master study [15]

Gender	Shame	Guilt	Externalization	Detachment	Alpha Pride	Beta Pride
Female	36.64	61.79	32.31	27.36	17.93	20.00
n=14	(9.12)	(6.84)	(9.07)	(6.71)	(2.64)	(2.45)
Male	37.00	54.81	33.29	27.90	16.45	17.32
n=31	(11.28)	(9.33)	(9.21)	(6.38)	(3.98)	(3.92)
Total	36.91	56.66	32.98	27.75	16.84	18.07
n=45	(10.67)	(9.01)	(9.18)	(6.48)	(3.67)	(3.71)

Table 14 compares male and female mean scores for urban youth from the Tangney and Dearing (2002) study, shelter youth from the pilot study, and shelter youth from the current study. Notably, the female mean guilt score for this master study was higher than for any other groups. Also notable was that the mean shame score for males in this group was higher than that for females of the same group. This was not the case for either of the other two groups. In many ways, scores for this group did not follow expectations. Because UPD, according to program reports, has seen a noteworthy increase in incidence of mental health issues, one might expect to see lower pride and guilt scores as these are associated, according to Tangney (1991), with a more balanced state of mental health. Based on this line of thinking it was also reasonable to expect higher shame, externalization, and detachment mean scores than in the population from the pilot study. This, in most instances, was not the case. The

---

[15] Standard deviation appears in parenthesis below mean. Shame, Guilt, and Externalization scores are derived from 15 items each, Detachment from 10 items, and Alpha and Beta Pride from five items each. Items are rated on a 5-point scale (1-5).

male mean shame score did follow this trend, but was exceptional in the way already mentioned. The female mean shame score was unexpectedly lower than the pilot score. Male and female mean guilt scores and mean pride scores were all higher than in the pilot study. Mean scores for externalization and male detachment were all, contrary to expectation, lower than in the pilot. The female mean detachment score followed expectations.

Table 14.

Mean scores for females and males from Tangney and Dearing (2002) study of urban youth, pilot study, and master study

	Shame	Guilt	Externalization	Detachment	Alpha Pride	Beta Pride
Urban Female	34.74	59.05	33.71	30.95	19.01	20.61
Urban Male	32.94	54.88	35.25	32.38	18.75	19.81
Pilot Female	37.58	55.50	34.25	25.83	16.92	18.83
Pilot Male	35.60	50.70	36.20	29.05	16.05	17.05
Master Study Female	36.64	61.79	32.21	27.36	17.93	20.00
Master Study Male	37.00	54.81	33.29	27.90	16.45	17.32

Figure 6 shows these scores graphed together. The lines do not diverge greatly from each other in five of the six scales measured by the TOSCA-A. The one scale where the mean scores differed most widely appears to be in guilt-proneness.

Figure 6. Comparison of Urban, Pilot, and Master Males and Females

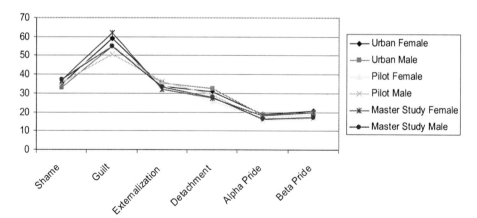

Since males and females tend to score differently in these six scales, it helps to see information for these groups broken out separately. Table 15 and Figure 7 provide this information for the female populations. Table 16 and Figure 8 provide it for the male populations. Differences between these combined male and female groups were that females tended to score higher in moral emotions and alpha and beta pride, while scoring lower in detachment and externalization. As previously mentioned, the mean shame score for master study males was the one instance where this did not hold true.

Table 15.

Mean scores for females from Tangney and Dearing (2002) study of urban youth, pilot study and master study

	Shame	Guilt	Externalization	Detachment	Alpha Pride	Beta Pride
Urban Female	34.74	59.05	33.71	30.95	19.01	20.61
Pilot Female	37.58	55.50	34.25	25.83	16.92	18.83
Master Study Female	36.64	61.79	32.21	27.36	17.93	20.00

Figure 7. Comparison of Urban, Pilot, and Master Study Females

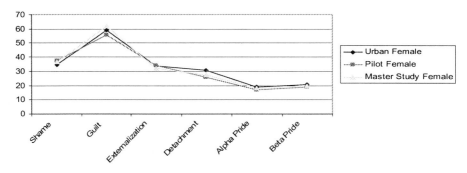

Table 16.

Mean scores for males from Tangney and Dearing (2002) study of urban youth, pilot study, and master study

	Shame	Guilt	Externalization	Detachment	Alpha Pride	Beta Pride
Urban Male	32.94	54.88	35.25	32.38	18.75	19.81
Pilot Male	35.60	50.70	36.20	29.05	16.05	17.05
Master Male	37.00	54.81	33.29	27.90	16.45	17.32

Figure 8. Comparison of Urban, Pilot, and Master Study Males

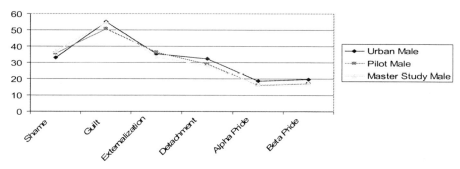

Table 17 combines males and females for each of the three populations. This was graphed in Figure 9. When males and females are combined in this way, the pilot and master populations follow each other very closely on four of six scales; the guilt-proneness and externalization scales being where they diverge most.

Table 17.

Mean scores for total populations from Tangney and Dearing (2002) study of urban youth[16], pilot study, and master study

	Shame	Guilt	Externalization	Detachment	Alpha Pride	Beta Pride
Urban Participants	33.96	57.24	34.38	31.57	18.90	20.26
Pilot Participants	36.34	52.50	35.47	27.84	16.38	17.72
Master Participants	36.89	56.98	32.96	27.73	16.91	18.16

Figure 9. Comparison of Urban, Pilot, and Master Total Populations

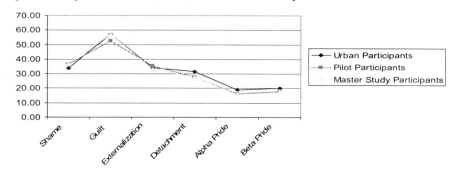

---

[16] Totals for Tangney et al. (2002) study were extrapolated from the separate data for male and female and were not actually included in the published work.

Table 18 and Figure 10 compare the Urban Youth study and combined homeless youth

groups. Using this larger sample of homeless youth, as might be expected, the mean shame

score was higher and mean guilt and pride scores were lower for the homeless population than

for the urban youth population. One might expect these youth to demonstrate more

externalization and detachment as a defense against experiencing the shameful self,

particularly in light of difficult circumstances in their lives.

Table 18.

Comparison of Urban and Homeless Youth (Pilot & Master Youth Combined)

	Shame	Guilt	Externalization	Detachment	Alpha Pride	Beta Pride
Urban Youth	33.96	57.24	34.38	31.57	18.90	20.26
Homeless Youth	36.46	55.10	33.92	27.94	16.69	18.03

Figure 10. Comparison of Urban and Homeless Youth

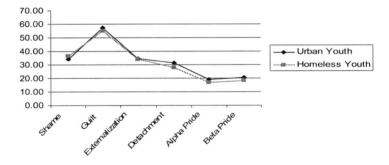

Focus Groups

As discussed previously, guilt-proneness scores determined participation in focus

groups. Participants with guilt-proneness scores one-half of a standard deviation above the

mean for their gender (scores of 66 or higher for females and 60 or higher for males) were

eligible for high guilt-proneness focus groups. Likewise, those with scores one-half of a

standard deviation below the mean for their gender (58 or lower for females and 50 or lower

for males) were eligible for low guilt-proneness focus groups. This yielded 14 potential participants for high-guilt-proneness groups (five females and nine males) and 13 potential

participants for low guilt-proneness groups (five females and eight males). Table 19 shows

mean TOSCA-A scores for high and low guilt-proneness groupings for all eligible

participants. Figure 11 compares mean scores for these two groups.

Table 19.

Master study – high and low mean guilt-proneness scores

	Shame	Guilt	Externalization	Detachment	Alpha Pride	Beta Pride
High Guilt-Proneness	38.79	66.64	29.70	27.00	17.00	19.50
Low Guilt-Proneness	32.38	47.38	32.60	26.80	15.54	15.46

Figure 11. Master study – high and low mean guilt-proneness scores

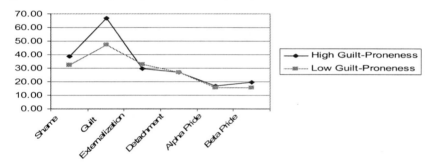

In addition to guilt-proneness scores being significantly higher for the high guilt-

proneness pool, beta pride scores were also significantly higher for these participants. While

the shame-proneness mean score was higher for the high guilt-proneness pool than for the low

guilt-proneness pool, it was not significantly higher, nor were there any other significant

differences between TOSCA-A scores for these groups. Table 20 shows t-test results with

values demonstrating a significant difference shown in bold. Degrees of freedom were 25 and

the two-tailed t-test value at .05 significance was 2.060.

Table 20.

T-test comparison of TOSCA-A scores of high and low guilt-proneness master pools

	Guilt	Shame	Externalization	Detachment	Alpha Pride	Beta Pride
Value of t	8.277	1.512	-.821	.089	.990	**3.107**

While facilitating focus groups, the principal investigator observed that youth in this study seemed less communicative and less able to remain focused on or go deeply into the topic than those in the pilot study. While this could be due, at least in part, to the different office situation of the principal investigator, it also seems appropriate to look at other factors that may have contributed to a difference. Table 21 shows mean TOSCA-A scores for high and low guilt-proneness groupings for the pilot study participants. These groupings were determined using one-half of standard deviation for the pilot study population's mean scores. Figure 12 compares mean scores for these two groups.

Table 21.

Pilot study – high and low mean guilt-proneness scores

	Shame	Guilt	Externalization	Detachment	Alpha Pride	Beta Pride
High Guilt-Proneness	37.46	62.54	31.50	23.30	17.08	18.77
Low Guilt-Proneness	21.25	37.88	36.40	30.80	13.63	14.00

Figure 12. Pilot study – high and low mean guilt-proneness scores

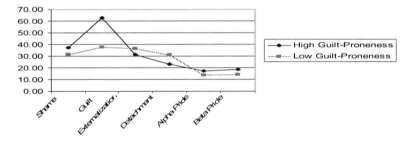

Two significant differences each were found when comparing the two high guilt-proneness pools and comparing the two low guilt-proneness pools. For the former, guilt-proneness scores were significantly higher for the master study high guilt-proneness pool. Table 22 shows that Externalization was also higher, but a significant difference was not clearly demonstrated. For the two low guilt-proneness groups, guilt-proneness was also significantly higher for the master study low guilt-proneness pool than for the pilot study pool and detachment was significantly lower for this master study pool than for the pilot study

pool. These differences will be explored later in the Discussion section. Tables 22 and 23

show statistical analysis of this comparison. Values of t that demonstrated a significant

difference are shown in bold. Degrees of freedom for the comparison between high guilt-

proneness groups were 25, with a two-tailed t-test value at a .05 significance of 2.060. For the

low guilt-proneness comparison, degrees of freedom were 19, with a two-tailed t-test value at

a .05 significance of 2.093.

Table 22.

T-test comparison of TOSCA-A scores of high guilt-proneness master and pilot study
participant pools

	Guilt	Shame	Externalization	Detachment	Alpha Pride	Beta Pride
Value of t	**2.791**	.272	2.059	-1.581	-.054	.692

Table 23.

T-test comparison of TOSCA-A scores of low guilt-proneness master and pilot study
participant pools

	Guilt	Shame	Externalization	Detachment	Alpha Pride	Beta Pride
Value of t	**2.611**	.287	.506	**-2.872**	1.084	.732

Table 24 shows mean TOSCA-A scores for focus groups in this study and the pilot

study. Figure 13 provides a graph of these scores as comparison.

Table 24.

Mean scores for master and pilot study focus groups

	Shame	Guilt	Externalization	Detachment	Alpha Pride	Beta Pride
High Guilt-Proneness Master Focus Group	38.33	67.17	30.70	26.20	17.17	19.33
Low Guilt-Proneness Master Focus Group	30.67	44.00	31.80	26.50	15.50	14.50
High Guilt-Proneness Pilot Focus Group	36.33	61.89	33.10	23.70	16.00	18.22

Figure 13. Mean scores - pilot and master study focus groups

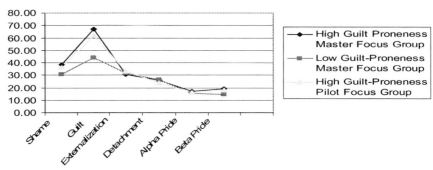

Comparing mean scores for master and pilot study high guilt-proneness focus groups, one significant difference was the master group was higher in guilt-proneness. The beta pride score was also significantly higher for this group. Table 25 shows t-test results with values demonstrating a significant difference shown in bold. Degrees of freedom were 10 and two-tailed t-test value at .05 significance was 2.228.

Table 25.

T-test comparison of TOSCA-A scores of high and low guilt-proneness master focus group participants

	Guilt	Shame	Externalization	Detachment	Alpha Pride	Beta Pride
Value of t	**9.883**	1.242	-.169	-.081	.750	**2.429**

Of the 27 potential participants, 12 took part in the focus groups. As previously stated, there was considerable difficulty with coordinating schedules, case plan demands, and willingness of the participants to be in the groups. Each group had three participants. Of the 12 participants, four (33%) were female and eight (66%) were male. The average age for males was slightly over 18 and for females was between 19 and 20. The ethnic breakdown was 42% Caucasian (one of whom was a male immigrant), 25% Black, 17% Multi-Racial, 8% Hispanic, and 8% Asian/Pacific Islander. The gender mix for the individual focus groups, including the principal investigator was: 50% male and 50% female for groups 1 and 3; 25%

male and 75% female for group 2; 75% male and 25% female for group 4. Groups 1 and 4 were low guilt-proneness groups; 2 and 3 were high guilt-proneness groups.

Group 1, a low guilt-proneness group, touched on many of the previous themes from the pilot study, though did not seem to do so to the depth of the pilot study groups. They also tended to stray from topic, the two males playing off of each other, using anecdotes of slapstick-like humor to avoid talking directly about their experience of remorse. There was also a tendency to stray toward blaming the system for such things as punishing victimless crimes, like smoking marijuana. While this group was gender-balanced, the male energy appeared dominant. The female was quiet, though strong in her opinions when she offered them. She tended to take a punitive and rigid stance regarding people who had done something wrong or had broken rules. One new remorse-invoking factor this group raised was a quality of innocence in the person who had been harmed. As will be discussed subsequently, two other groups echoed the importance of this.

This group spoke strongly about physical aspects of remorse. They firmly stated their belief that remorse was something that could be seen in a remorseful person's eyes if it was truly there and could not be faked. They also talked about experiencing remorse as if one has "dropped from a height and landed flat; it was a sickening feeling." Another suggestion was the emotion was so strong in its negativity it makes one feel physically ill.

Their other comments touched on several of the pilot study themes. Similarly to the pilot study group, they thought the words "I'm sorry" were overused and, therefore, meaningless unless accompanied by actions and behaviors that signify a change. This discussion did not reach the level of a major life-changing transformation, though in the later discussion about innocence, it did begin to move there. They also believed it was very important that someone directly take responsibility for their harmful action. Remorse is not credible if the person does not come face-to-face with the victim to admit what was done, apologize, and make amends. It did not matter how long it took for this to happen, but it was critical that it happen. Additionally, they spoke about remorse as having a sense of hopelessness, powerlessness; this came up in the context of an immediate reaction after commission of the act. They also said that depression could result from remorse. This was similar to Tangney's description of a shame response, rather than a guilt response, but walks that line of the dilemma that, while remorse can lead to reparation, the harm truly cannot be undone. Another way of looking at this, however, was that without the remorse-inducing incident, potential growth and transformation might not be attained, and this was where hope of remorse lies. Unlike the pilot group discussion, this was not the nature of remorse that this group articulated.

It was in the discussion of harm to innocence that the other themes of importance of relatedness, intentionality, and severity of harm emerged to a small degree. One of the youth told a story of having stolen money from his 7-year old brother. He expressed deep regret for this, and another participant demonstrated understanding of how awful this feeling must be. The youth was not willing to share what his little brother said to him when they spoke after the theft was revealed. He stated that he did not want to think about it, but that their relationship was okay now. The unwillingness to think about the conversation could be seen as a shame response, in that he wanted to hide from the memory and feelings by not thinking about them or sharing them. The primary focus of the story was that the youth did not want to repeat such an act due to the awfulness of the feelings, but little focus was placed on what, if anything, he did to make amends for the harm. When asked if this would have been as important for him if it had been another little boy who was not his brother, the discussion indicated that the harm to innocence was still very important as inducement to remorse, but not quite as much as when there was a sense of relatedness with the victim. The discussion then moved to severity of harm, indicating that if the money had not been a meaningful amount to the victim, then remorse would be reduced. On this point, one member did express that stealing was stealing and still required punishment. When the group was asked if the harm had been something unintentional, would the feelings be as strong, the response indicated that there would be serious attempts to repair the harm or help the victim, but they would not be "sent into the depths of depression." It seems in this instance that the shame response would not be triggered for them and that reparation would be primary.

When speaking about shame-inducing events, very little was said about what other people think of them in these instances. This seems to point to an internal quality of shame, meaning, contrary to some thought that shame was primarily about being seen by others as despicable, being seen by one's own internal judge as despicable was quite painful. One can still feel the blush of shame without being in the presence of others.

The final part of this group's discussion that was on topic was remorse for harm to self, or not realizing one's potential. This concept elicited a response of self-rejection, but also a story from one youth of having to work very hard to regain access to services at UPD. Previous behavior had resulted in the youth being restricted from all services. The youth expressed a deep sense of having harmed himself and the trust of the staff and stated that he had to work very hard to have his service restriction lifted.

The group ended by straying toward the "slap-stick" humor stories and finally by talking at length about how the system penalizes people for victim-less crimes while rapists and men who physically abuse their wives can go unpunished. Looking at this tendency, it was noteworthy that these trends in the discussion not only correlate well with the significantly lower guilt and pride scores of the low guilt-proneness groups, but also display both detachment and externalization. Interestingly, this group had the lowest mean externalization score and the second lowest mean detachment score of the four groups. Meaning, there did not appear to be a straight-forward correlation between these TOSCA-A scores and information gathered in focus group discussion.

Group 2 was a high guilt-proneness group. This group readily remained focused on the topic. The dynamics of this group were such that one female was very verbal, while the two other participants, one male and one female, were quieter in varying degrees. This group also raised a new concept in describing remorse by talking about someone's physical appearance, demeanor, and attire. Although in the minority from the perspective of gender, the male did actively participate, though at times the facilitator had to make room for both of the quieter participants to speak. This group also stated that for true remorse, behavior had to change. Further, remorse would be most evident by looking into someone's eyes, and that harm to innocence was a remorse-inducing factor. Remorse is also something that leaves the remorseful person feeling as if they can never completely make reparation for the harm they caused. Like group 1 of this study, they too thought that "I'm sorry" was a much overused phrase, unless the person can also articulate why he or she was sorry. Even more importantly, the behavior must change or not be repeated. They also saw, as did Group 3, that there was value in getting to a place of remorse and articulating it, even if the other person did not believe you were truly remorseful. There was a sense of taking responsibility, paying back the debt, and even if it was not recognized or valued, that one would be better for it. This recognizes an intrinsic value to remorse, even if extrinsic rewards, in this case forgiveness from the other, are absent from the outcome. What the group was split over was self-forgiveness. Both female participants struggled with feeling, not only self-forgiveness, but also self-esteem. One female specifically stated that she did not feel deserving and could not forgive herself. The male was much more able to accept that he could not change action he had taken, that we all "screw up," and it was a matter of forgiving oneself and not doing it again. A question worth pursuing is whether or not moving away from shame toward remorse and reparation requires self-forgiveness.

Regarding innocence and forgiveness, this group spoke at length about their younger siblings and girlfriends toward whom they felt protective and they felt angry toward parents who were harming them in some way. They were less forgiving in this case. One comment that was very telling of the hurt they had seen and experienced was, "If you can't have remorse, then you shouldn't have children."

When asked how they would view it if the harm were unintentional, their response was that it would take a while to get to a place of feeling remorse. This would be particularly true if they did not understand or could not empathize with the person who was harmed. One participant used an example of having unknowingly caused a financial dilemma which resulted in her family being evicted from their home. It took a while for her to understand and grow to be remorseful in this situation.

In addition to the eyes being an indicator of remorse, this group spoke of appearance, dress, and demeanor as well. This included being aware of colors people choose to wear, words they choose to use (e.g., "cussing" or teasing unkindly), and general self-presentation or how one carries oneself (e.g., over-assuredness or acting privileged). They believed these things would change if a person were truly remorseful.

They also spoke of a sense of hopelessness and helplessness, again in Tangney's terms, more of a shame response. The male participant commented that everyone has remorse, but it was just hard to "follow through with what you need to do." Depression, anger, and frustration can get in the way of getting to remorse. A clear example of more functional coping skills than the low guilt-proneness groups articulated or demonstrated was when one youth stated that he uses painting, walking, and poetry as an outlet for these negative feelings, instead of choosing to hurt other people. He further suggested that sometimes it was hard to get to remorse because people cannot bear to hear the truth, because it hurts. Fear gets in the way. This agrees with Henderson et al. (2001), who suggest a link between shame, fear, private self-consciousness, and social anxiety. Their work suggests that this can result in withdrawal from the situation rather than an ability to move toward it in a reparative manner. One female participant told a story of lying to her mother about things that she was doing and her current situation. This seemed to be quite painful and difficult for her to discuss. She expressed desire for a way to be more honest with her mother, and to feel safe in doing so. Another comment was that when remorse was present, there was pain; if it was not, then there was no pain. If the remorseful person does not get lost in feeling pain, then the person can make some reparation and then will feel better. You feel better when you make reparation, but you can still regret the action.

Group 3, also a high guilt-proneness group, had balanced dynamics regarding participation, though individual perspectives varied widely at times. Two concepts that were uniquely stressed by this group were empathy and forgiveness. One male had a strong punitive attitude that came out in a belief that he did not experience remorse because he was careful to be sure any action against someone was a justifiable action. He believed individuals, inclusive of him, needed consequences in order to learn upon the first offense that a behavior was unacceptable. Later in the discussion, he did contradict himself by stating that when he does do something harmful he thinks about the situation, how it started, and how to fix it or move on without doing it again. He further offered that apology is important, not to make himself feel better, but to let others know that he was sorry. Though he did not articulate it specifically, his stated concern was to meet the needs of the person rather than assuage his guilt or meet his self-esteem needs. In Lazare's view (2004), if he wanted to be successful in this, he would need to assure that his apology attended to such needs as restoring the relationship, making it safe again, and assuring the other person that it was not their fault. This youth also raised the concept of innocence. He did this with an example of a shelter client, who was learning disabled and had a very disarming demeanor. If this client harmed him, he would know that this person "comes from the heart" and did not intend the harm and, therefore, would not deserve the consequence. In line with the concept of innocence, this group, like group 2, talked about harm to someone, such as a baby brother or sister, being remorse inducing.

This group touched on empathy when they stated that each of them was in a difficult situation in their lives. If they got mad or hurt each other, they stepped back and realized that they were all operating from a challenging situation. Thus, they established the sense of relatedness that Shaw (1989) sees as important for remorse to arise. They would feel remorseful about lashing out at or being judgmental of others in similar life circumstances. They talked about understanding that, while they all have difficulties, they each are different and have lived different lives. So, appreciating a different perspective, or empathizing, allowed them to experience remorse and forgiveness.

When asked about intentional harm, they again turned to empathy for each other's difficult circumstances. They saw the importance of setting aside anger for petty offenses, particularly if they were unintentional, since they had much larger problems to consider. One youth stated, "I don't expect people here to feel remorse for me in their lives. They have big enough things in their lives; I don't need to be another big thing for them."

Regarding physical aspects of remorse, the group came from varied perspectives. One thought that it was all thinking, another that there was possibility of it being a physical experience, and the third was clearly aware of a physical experience of remorse. They talked about seeing it in a person's eyes or a serious look, a sickening or dead feeling, and emotions so strong that it made them ill. The one who spoke of "coming from the heart" earlier in the discussion was adamant that remorse was purely a thought process, again a contradiction for this youth. This seemed to indicate this youth's difficulty with connecting with his emotions, or with being vulnerable in this group.

Describing remorse, they spoke of it as knowing what you did was wrong and "putting" it in such a way (either actions or words) that the other person can see that you are sorry. By this, you make yourself, and the other person, feel better by "owning up to what you did." Other phrases included, "being truly sorry for what you did" and "forgiving or having someone else forgive you." So, for them, it seems, remorse was inextricably tied to forgiveness. This was further supported when they were asked to provide final thoughts on remorse and they stated that forgiving summed it up for them. They also offered that remorse

107

was both about the future and the past, but not living in the past. It was mostly about the future, because they wanted the harm to be fixed.

Group 4 was a low guilt-proneness group. Of all the groups, this one had the most difficulty with the topic. While one participant attempted to be supportive of the discussion, the other two participants were very reticent. One of the reluctant participants did share a story of a friend who was angry at him for leaving him who, in his anger, burned all the participant's belongings. The participant heard second-hand that his friend was sorry, but this apology did not seem completely credible to him because it was not made directly and there was no reparation. Another participant talked about visiting his family during the time scheduled for his GED graduation ceremony. He regretted not attending, but failed to do so because his family did not want to go. The group also offered some description of remorse as being truly sorry and apologetic, wanting to repair harm, and not repeating the behavior. This was the extent of the substance of the discussion that related directly to the topic.

While the other low guilt-proneness group found that humor was a useful tool for avoidance, the two members who had difficulty with the topic seemed simply to shut down. This indicated for the facilitator that these youth did not have a defense mechanism that provided them with a vehicle to stay engaged, while still avoiding the painful topic. It seemed that the strength and stability of their ego-structure was even less than that of the first low guilt-proneness group. When one youth stated that the topic was too painful for him to talk about because of things he had done, the facilitator shifted off topic and turned the discussion to some of their case plan successes, such as skills classes, passing GED classes, job search techniques, and other program services available to them. To wrap up, the facilitator returned to topic by briefly talking about remorse for loss of their potential if they did not continue making efforts in their case plans and commended them for their efforts. They were also encouraged to talk with their case managers if they had any disturbing thoughts or feelings resulting from the discussion.

As stated previously, all participants signed a consent form indicating that if the facilitator felt concern for the youth, such concern would be raised with appropriate program staff. At the end of the group, the facilitator notified the case manager and shelter counselor on duty that it was a difficult topic for the group. She asked these staff to maintain awareness and check in with the youth if they noticed any problems. They later reported that, in discussions with the youth over the course of the evening, they felt reassured about the three participants.

The events of this group may relate to low guilt-proneness scores, the lowest mean score of all four groups, and the fact that as a group they also had lowest mean alpha and beta pride scores and second highest shame score. Another dynamic which may have influenced the outcome was that all participants were male. Without a peer female to allow them to access softer emotions and still "save face" while setting aside male bravado, they could not fully enter the discussion. Additionally, unlike the pilot focus group that was all male, the facilitator had only limited rapport with the individual youth in this group. The one participant who was able to be most supportive of the discussion was the only one with whom the facilitator had previously had one-on-one conversation. It was possible these factors, as well as other unknown factors, influenced the outcome.

In summary, there were many similarities between concepts raised by both the high guilt-proneness and low guilt-proneness groups. The concept of innocence came up in the three groups that were able to discuss the topic for the full hour, as did the experience of remorse being a physical one, the importance of relatedness to the victim, and discussion of some type of shame response like fear or embarrassment. Across all four groups, a meaningful apology was stressed as important. Along with this apology, there must be some direct contact, articulation of an understanding of the harm caused, and reparation for the harm. Other topics discussed in various groups, without necessarily being linked to guilt-proneness scores, were: self-rejection; a sense of irrevocable harm, resulting in hopelessness and powerlessness; importance of intentionality; some ability to access remorse for self; repairing harm to self; and importance of severity of loss.

Differences for high guilt-proneness versus low guilt-proneness were fewer than similarities, but, particularly in the case of group 4, strongly apparent. High guilt-proneness groups were much more able to remain focused on the topic without distracting through humor or by shutting down. High guilt-proneness focus group participants were also generally more able to articulate self-forgiveness, if not necessarily maintain a posture of self-forgiveness. They also articulated thoughts about lack of remorse when actions were justifiable, the intrinsic rewards and value of remorse, the impact of shame responses on their ability to access remorse, and an implied connection between empathy and remorse. There was only one group, Group 1, which thought that severity of loss to the victim was an important factor for inducing remorse. TOSCA-A scores may offer some insight into these differences. While high guilt-proneness groups had higher shame-proneness scores than low guilt-proneness groups, it was possible that the combination of significantly higher guilt-proneness scores and beta pride scores provide them with self-esteem that allows them to move from shame, or I am bad, to guilt, which was more about I did a bad thing. This is something to be explored further in discussion of the individual case studies.

Individual Case Studies

To score the PFQ - - 2, mean scores for the six items relating to guilt and the ten items relating to shame were determined. Mean scores of 2 or more were considered high. Shame scores for the case study group trended in the same direction as individual shame scores on the TOSCA-A shame. On the other hand, there was no apparent straight-forward pattern that tied PFQ - - 2 guilt scores to the guilt or shame scales of the TOSCA-A or any other measures of the TOSCA-A. This observation supports Tangney's stance that the guilt scale of the PFQ - - 2 and that of the TOSCA-A do not measure the same thing. Additionally, when Henderson et al. (2001) used this instrument, they used it as a measure of state, rather than trait by changing the directions from, "indicate how common the feeling is for you" to "indicate how much you feel this way right now." Henderson, however, was using the tool to study shame and, as shown in Table 25, the two shame scales do show similar trends.

Table 26.

TOSCA-A and PFQ - - 2 scores for case study participants

	TOSCA-A						PFQ - - 2	
Name	Shame	Guilt	Externalization	Detachment	Beta Pride	Alpha Pride	Shame	Guilt
Linda	23	67	14	14	17	21	1.2	1.5
Steve	25	44	26	24	17	15	1.3	2.5
William	42	44	37	50	14	18	2.1	2.0
Ingrid	51	69	33	38	21	20	2.9	2.5

The TAT was scored using the spreadsheet in Appendix D. TAT sessions were tape-recorded for purposes of recall and accuracy. For these individual case studies, the principal investigator used the multiple facets of the study to gain understanding of the individual's experience of remorse and apparent influencing factors of that experience. These facets include the seven factors examined in the statistical survey, TOSCA-A and PFQ - - 2 results, case history and notes, and information gathered through administration of the TAT. Richness

of the data elicited by the TAT allows any number of interpretations, depending upon which

aspect of the data one focuses. While one criticism of the TAT is the large number of scoring

systems, this is also a strength, because one would expect to score it differently depending

upon focus of the research. Murray himself sought to find the individuality of each person,

rather than the similarities between people (Anderson, 1999). Because this study is based in

an existential-humanistic and transpersonal epistemology, it was vital that, like Murray, it

focus upon the whole person's experience of remorse. Therefore, evaluation of TAT

responses was recorded similarly to Bellak's approach, and yet was tailored to remorse and

related themes.

Case Study 1, Linda, defined remorse as feeling deeply that what you did was wrong

and speaking or acting in a way that clearly let the person who was harmed know that you

understood how they were harmed and that you are sorry. She was 19 years old and declared

herself as a heterosexual, Hispanic woman. She had two identified psychosocial factors,

histories of being physically abused and of substance abuse. She was in Focus Group 3, a high

guilt-proneness score group. The reason for choosing her for an individual case study was an

incident she related with another shelter youth. In this incident she was involved in a fight

with a female friend in the shelter. The fight resulted from gossip that Linda helped

perpetuate. Her friend was physically attacked by a third female because of the gossip and,

Linda, realizing her contribution to the conflict, stepped in to defend her friend; both she and

her friend were injured in the altercation. This brought her to the realization that all youth at

UPD are in similarly difficult circumstances and that, because of this, she felt remorse for

instigating the conflict.

In 2000, Linda was in a group home for three months and then in a residential treatment center for substance abuse for one month. While she does report having partied excessively in the past, she states that she avoids this activity now. She states that her father was abusive to her as a child and she moved into a marriage with a man who was also physically abusive. Having grown up in this type of environment, she believed at one time that this was just the way it was. Once she realized this was not right, she extricated herself from this abusive relationship, moved in with friends, and has been working toward stabilizing her living situation. She came to UPD looking for assistance with this in July 2004, after her friends asked her to leave their home. As far as finding employment, she stood in good stead compared to many of her contemporaries in the shelter. Linda was bright, well-spoken, had her GED, and was trained in a number of basic skills such as construction work, retail, and cashiering. She gained many of these skills through Job Corps. In August of 2004, Linda realized UPD could not help her with her housing situation in the way that she hoped and has not been seen at UPD since then.

While Linda described herself as very social, her group of close friends was small and she considered her main support system to include her mother, with whom she had very strained relations, and her best friend. Linda tended to get involved in the intensity of the social dynamics of the shelter[17] and sometimes found herself acting as loyal defender of those in her social group. She also exhibited some other care-taking tendencies, such as fixing and cutting hair for the other youth.

Linda's responses to the TAT showed several repeating themes. A dominant theme was overbearing and punitive parent to child relationships, primarily relating to a mother

---

[17] The shelter serves 35-45 youth, generally between the ages of 17 and 21, each day and night. This service occurs in very limited space and many of the youth have mental health issues, substance abuse issues, and other psychosocial issues that affect social interactions with each other. This is in addition to the emotional and energetic intensity that young people this age typically experience. The youth refer to this dynamic as "the drama of the shelter."

rather than a father. There was also a theme of unsuccessful male and female relationships, such as mother with son and husband with wife. Frequently, when the heroine of the story engaged in an angry or negative behavior, Linda spoke of an outcome in which the individual would rethink his or her behavior, or position in choosing that behavior, and decide that there was perhaps another, better, way of acting or thinking. At one point she followed such an outcome by saying, "what you want to do and what you should do are two different things." Themes of guilt-proneness appeared more often than did shame-related themes, such as the hero or heroine wanting to hide from the situation.

Linda also demonstrated a clear tendency toward empathizing with people in her stories. In debriefing after completing the TAT, Linda stated that, while some pictures left her with little to say, many of them brought back memories with her family; memories she had not thought of in a long time. Particularly reminiscent of her past was the picture of the woman reading with the young girl with the doll who was disinterested. This brought back memories of the many times when Linda's mother would insist she read with her. Linda stated that she enjoyed reading with her brothers and grandparents, but not with her mother. She further stated that her mother frequently grounded her for things she did as a child. She saw her own behavior and her mother's unfairness, such as blaming her for her older brother's choice to move away from home, as the source of this consequence. She seemed to feel some hurt that remained from this blaming, but expressed understanding that her behavior was also a problem. There was little evidence that she experienced this as a reflection of who she was, but rather, of what she did.

Case Study 2, William, saw remorse as when you take responsibility for your actions that harmed someone else by apologizing and fixing the problem. He shared that he was a 19 year-old newly immigrated[18] young man who identified as heterosexual. He had no identified psychosocial issues. William was in Focus Group 4, a low guilt-proneness score group. He was chosen for the individual case study because his willingness to try to support the discussion during the focus group demonstrated that he would have the ego strength to be a part of this phase without placing him under harmful stress. In conversations with the principal investigator, William also shared some concerns with the circumstances in his native country which had created a great deal of painful separation for his family members and he spoke of deep regret for leaving much of his family behind. The principal investigator felt that this satisfied the requirement of a personally meaningful story of remorse.

William came to UPD in April of 2004 after his stepfather gave him an ultimatum to either join the Navy or move out. Although William completed high school in his native country he chose to also complete his GED in English. He hoped to also become a citizen and was practicing for the test. William was friendly, but did not seem to connect deeply with any of the other youth. He also had a dry sense of humor, which combined with his very thick accent, can completely take people by surprise or leave them wondering if he really meant to joke. He also worked to pick up slang that other youth use. He was determined to assimilate into this culture, refusing to seek support or services from the community of people from his native country.

William clearly expressed hurt and shame about his circumstances, but through his body language and tone, not in his words. He looked down with a sad face when talking about the ostracism from his family. His stepfather kept William's mother from having much contact with her son. He was also embarrassed to be homeless, and when seeking work had

---

[18] Revealing the country from which William immigrated, would likely make him easily identified by any Urban Peak staff that might read this study, and therefore has not been done.

been coached to hide this because some places would not hire people in such circumstances. William had a disadvantage in finding employment with his thick accent, but his speech had become much clearer over the past six months. He had also learned new skills, such as forklift operation, and hoped to continue this effort by going into Job Corps. Unfortunately, due to lack of cooperation from his parents, he had trouble getting proper documentation to get into this program. After many months of searching, William was hired at a convenience store, where he worked the night shift. He was very pleased that he had found employment, but shared his concern that he had to lie about his place of residence. He claimed that he still lived at his parents's home. He expressed concern that they would fire him for falsifying his information if they found out and, if not for that, then for being homeless. A fortunate turn was that within a few weeks of holding this employment he had enough money to put a down payment on an apartment at one of the UPD apartment facilities. He truly was now no longer homeless.

During the TAT, William again used his delightful dry sense of humor, possibly to deflect any emotion he might be experiencing. One example was with Card 5, in which a woman was looking into a room with a look of surprise or dismay on her face. Like the other youth, he interpreted this as a mother who was checking in on her children to see what they were doing. William first stated that the children had broken the fish tank, then that they had their hands in the fish tank. Then he decided that the children had put the cat in the fish tank. There were several times when he seemed to, conspiratorially, make fun of the picture or process, waiting for the principal investigator to catch on.

With a few exceptions, he did not seem to allow himself to have a deep sense of the emotions he spoke about. He looked into the faces of the people in the pictures and, on his own admission, stated that sometimes he had nothing to say because he could not see emotion in their faces. One picture that seemed particularly poignant for him was 13B. This was the little boy sitting on the doorstep of a log cabin. William commented upon the boy's bare feet. He stated that the house was not a rich one and that the boy would clearly have to work very hard to make his life good. The boy, it seemed, had no shoes or, if he did, he only had one or two pairs that he saved for holidays, church, or school. The boy did not have a good relationship with his parents. Regarding Card 14, the silhouette of a person by a bright window, William made an interesting comment. He stated that it was a boy looking at the stars and the boy was dreaming about himself and he was a romantic. Yet another picture that seemed revealing was the interpretation of the Card 6BM. In this card a woman was standing next to a window with her back to a man who appears to be frowning and looking down. William saw this as a man and his mother. She felt sad and he felt guilty because they did not understand each other. William thought that they were not angry yet, but did not feel good and that they should come together and care about each other. These seemed to offer insight into William's feelings about himself and his current circumstances, and possibly also alluded to some past experiences or things he witnessed previously.

Additionally, William offered some empathic interpretations for pictures whose main character was female. The first was for Card 3GF. In this card a woman holds a door with one hand with her head in her other hand as she seemed to be leaving a room. William suggested that she would become or was hysterical and, in this state, she might begin to cry loudly and throw things. He surmised that she had lost something. Optimistically, he stated that the outcome would be that she would find or replace whatever it was that she had lost, which he stated could be her keys, job, or boyfriend. When asked if he thought she blamed herself for the loss, he stated pretty definitely that she did not blame herself. In another example of being able to empathize with feminine figures, Card 7GF where a woman reads while a young girl looking off, inattentively, holds a doll, William saw this doll as a real baby. He said that while the woman was reading and not paying attention to the girl, the girl, likewise, was dreaming up stories in her head and not paying attention to the baby.

Of particular note was the story told in response to Card 6BM. This story of "a man and his mother" reflected moral emotions that could be interpreted as guilt and remorse. In this story the son felt guilty because he and his mother did not understand each other and William thought they should find a way to reach each other and care about each other. This could well reflect the current situation of alienation from his own mother through her marriage to his step-father. He also said that the son and mother were not angry with each other yet, but it did not feel good, the implication being that if they did not find a way to care, this could turn into anger.

For the most part, William's stories implied cognitive understanding of why the subjects of the stories might have been experiencing emotionally. In the stories, it was clear that William might have been reflecting some of his own life experience, particularly regarding himself and his mother. He did not, however, in the telling seem very emotionally engaged himself. He told the stories very dryly, sometimes slipping into humor, possibly as a way to deflect emotional experience. This seems to correlate well with William's very high score, 50, in the area of detachment. He also had a fairly high score of 37 in externalization. So, it does not seem surprising that he would tell his stories of emotion without demonstrating emotional engagement.

Case Study 3, Ingrid believes that remorse requires not only an apology but the ability to articulate the specifics of the harm that was done. This shows that the person who did the harmful action is able to empathetically understand the harm that was caused. Ingrid Participated in Group 2, a high guilt-proneness group. She had the highest guilt and shame scores of the case study group. This was true both for the TOSCA-A and PFQ - - 2. Ingrid was a 20 year-old woman who declared herself as heterosexual and of Asian descent. Ingrid's case history showed two identified psychosocial issues, mental health (primarily, depression) and physical abuse. Ingrid was chosen for this study because of a story she shared during the focus group about how she has deceived her parents, having engaged in smoking and use of alcohol and drugs, when she had told them that she was not doing this. She seemed to have a deep sense of regret about this.

Ingrid was born in Colorado and lived with her parents, older sister, and younger brother. She graduated from high school in June of 2002 and was asked to leave home in November of that year due to disagreements with her father, the final one being about her addiction to cigarettes. She moved around, living with friends, until their hospitality was no longer available to her. She came to UPD in April of 2003. The next month, Ingrid reunited with her mother, unknown to her father, and her mother revealed that she was planning to leave her father because he was abusive and controlling with her. Ingrid chose not to reveal her homelessness to her mother. Over the next few months, Ingrid stayed in touch with her mother while she, somewhat unenthusiastically, sought employment so she could qualify for one of UPD's apartments. During this time she was diagnosed with major depression and began medication. Though Ingrid feared leaving the support of the shelter, she found employment and moved to an apartment. She was honored as client of the week for this accomplishment. Shortly afterward, she lost her employment, began to defy client rules at the apartment complex, was restricted repeatedly from UPD services because of her choice not to follow her program, forged a check to pay rent, and, by June of 2004, lost her apartment and was back in the shelter on a full-time basis. Subsequently, Ingrid focused more on her job search, was published several times in a youth newspaper, and was an active participant in UPD's youth council.[19] She, most recently, became interested in going to college. She continued to have contact with her mother, but did not tell her mother she lived at a homeless shelter.

Ingrid's demeanor during the TAT administration was low energy and soft spoken, as it was in the focus group. Ingrid summarized these pictures as all being about happiness, sadness, or frustration. The most revealing story Ingrid shared was about Card 6BM. She said this was a son and his mother. The son has lied to his mother and she was disappointed in him. Interestingly, she stated that he already regrets what he did, but in the future he would realize that it was wrong. This perhaps was representative of Ingrid's current situation of regretting her lies to her parents about smoking, drug use, and being homeless, but, simultaneously, continuing to hide the fact of her homelessness from them. This seems to match with Ingrid's high guilt and shame scores. She had regrets and seemed to want to address them, but was still very much caught in the shame of her circumstances and perhaps fearful of how her parents would respond to the truth if she told them. In addition to this story, the general themes for Ingrid regarding parental relationships were ones of neglect, lack of understanding, and disappointment.

---

[19] The youth council is part of UPD's approach to working with youth through a philosophy of youth development that encourages partnering with them in bringing them the services they need. Youth council discusses shelter issues and makes recommendations to staff regarding how these issues can be resolved. They also help facilitate creative and educational activities for the youth.

120

A second story in which Ingrid addressed regret was one she told for Card 8BM. She stated that the figure in the foreground was the same person as the one who was on the operating table. This foreground figure was a ghost watching doctors take his organs for donation. Ingrid described the young man as being angry and having deep regrets about being dead because there was much more that he could have done with his life. She said, "He could have lived a lot more." When asked how the young man died, she stated that it was either because of an accident caused by his own error, or by gunshot.

Ingrid also had fairly high Alpha and Beta Pride scores. She was the only one who spoke of pride in one of her stories. For Card 14, she stated that this figure was either a boy or a girl posing for an artist and that he or she had a healthy sense of pride. This story could reflect Ingrid's own aspirations as an artist through her poetry.

Case study 4, Steve was very skeptical about apologies and was unlikely to accept "I'm sorry" without actions that not only repaired the damage, but also went one step beyond. For example in the case of something being stolen, true remorse, for Steve, meant the person replaced it with more than was taken. Steve believed that remorse looked different for everyone, but one key piece was that the behavior should never be repeated. He was 20 years old and identified as multi-racial. Steve also questioned his sexuality. He participated in Focus Group 1, a low guilt-proneness group. Steve's case history showed two identified psychosocial issues, substance abuse and mental health issues. Steve was chosen for this case study based upon the story he told regarding his regrets about losing the trust of UPD staff and his efforts to regain that trust. Unfortunately, as of the date of this writing, Steve had again lost his services due to difficulty he had in following through on his case plan.

Steve was born in Colorado and, prior to coming to UPD, lived in a relatively affluent neighborhood in a suburb of Denver. In spite of this, Steve's life was difficult for him; between the ages of 9 and 12 he attempted suicide seven times. By age 16 when he began driving, he incurred numerous traffic citations. He was enrolled in special education classes due to his behavioral problems and had to repeat his senior year because he was short a few credits. He did not complete high school. Instead he moved into an apartment with friends after being asked to leave his parents's home. Unable to sustain employment, he became homeless, arriving at UPD in April 2003. Steve made good progress in his first month by completing his GED, opening conversations with his parents, and gaining their support in resolving his legal issues for defacing private property (tagging) and mischief, and completing traffic school. The following month, however, Steve began to destabilize as his case manager prepared to leave on a sabbatical. He was involved in a fight that resulted in his hospitalization. His parents responded by having him come home briefly. The downward trend continued as he was assigned to a new case manager, was caught smoking marijuana, and also was not following through on case plan commitments. His case manager and parents met with him and though he made renewed commitments to his case plan, he still did not follow through and was restricted from UPD services in August 2003.

In January of 2004, Steve contacted UPD and requested access to services. This was denied based on the belief that he was supplying illegal substances to other UPD youth. During this period of restriction Steve lived with his parents on and off, or with friends, and occasionally had phone contact with UPD staff. In August 2004, he requested services once again and was allowed to return. He wanted to find employment and begin exploring the option of going to college. He also hoped to move into an apartment. He dropped by to tell the principal investigator that he had found employment, but this seemed tenuous and his demeanor still seemed lethargic and depressed. Ultimately, in spite of staff attempts to support him, he was unable to maintain focus on his plans for himself. Additionally, drug paraphernalia was found in his belongings, after which he was once again restricted from services as of the end of September 2004.

Steve began the TAT wanting to know what the right or normal response was to the pictures. After some reassurance that he could take the freedom to tell his own story, he allowed himself to indulge his imagination. Most notable was his keen attention to details that others had not noticed in the pictures. While this could be interpreted as hyper-vigilance, it might also be because he was still searching for clues for the right answer. For example, in Card 3BM, he was the only case study participant to notice the object on the floor to the left of the figure. He thought it might be keys or a pack of cigarettes and did not recognize it as a gun. Steve's ability to empathize with people in the pictures was strong. He seemed very emotionally engaged with feelings in the stories he told. Of the four case studies, both he and Linda were the most emotionally engaged in their stories and this seems to relate to the fact that they also had detachment scores below the norm. The most telling theme in Steve's stories was how the subjects of them were surprised and saddened by consequences of their actions. They did not quite move to remorse or reparation, but experienced great pain in payment for their actions. This was particularly true in Cards 3GF and 6BM. In the first of these, the woman was walking away from something she needed to deal with and she realized that she should have dealt with it sooner, because she was now suffering with "intense sorrow" and was facing "incredible consequences." Nevertheless, something was holding her back from dealing with it; "maybe she is holding herself back." In the third card mentioned,

Steve, again spoke about the seriousness of consequences that perhaps the two people in the picture could have done something to prevent. The man, Steve said, knew more about what happened than the woman. While the man fidgeted with his hat (another example of a detail that Steve noticed that no one else mentioned), he was thinking about what he could have done differently. Steve also said that there was something secretive about the man's behavior with the woman and he wondered why it had to be that way.

There was a theme of difficult communications (the nature of them being unkind, secretive, or rife with misunderstanding) between women and children and women and men. Another such example was the response to Card 5. In this story, a mother was entering a room to tell the children, in a very spiteful manner, (he likened her to "an evil step-mother") they should not be doing what they were doing and should know better.

Two stories that offered additional insight were told in response to Cards 13BM and 15. In the first, he actually placed himself in the story stating that his car had broken down in the middle of nowhere and he was walking up to the boy sitting in the doorway. The boy would not help him because his parents had left him home alone with instruction that no visitors were allowed. It seemed that Steve could have been both the boy and the visitor in this story. In being the boy, he was left home alone by his parents with a rule that did not seem to make sense, and resulted in confounding what he, as the visitor, needed in the situation. The next step in this explanation could also be that Steve, as both characters in this story, perceived that he was powerless to help himself. In Card 15, Steve talked about the old man as very sad and feeling his own mortality (perdition was the actual word he used). The man was also feeling responsible for a lot of death. Feeling cursed by it, he wondered why some people have to die.

124

In all these stories Steve seemed to say that he felt the heavy weight of his difficult relationship with his parents, his mother primarily, and he felt very responsible for his circumstances and felt regret, but did not know what to do about it. He seemed to say that he was caught by rules and parents that did not make sense to him or that may not have his best interest in mind and that consequences he suffered were far more than he expected and more, perhaps, than he thought he deserved. Before he lost his services, the principal investigator and he had a conversation about a job he had through the father of another youth. He was outraged that his case manager was not taking this job seriously and giving him credit he felt was due. He was blaming her for not seeing its value, rather than recognizing that he had perhaps taken a job that was tenuous in nature. He later lost the job due to an argument with his boss, his friend's father. This behavior may be an example of Tangney's and Dearing's (2002) discussion of how shame can transmute to self-righteous anger in an effort to keep the bad self and shame hidden.

CHAPTER 6. DISCUSSION

For this final section it is important to provide a reminder that the larger context of this study is restorative justice and remorse for this population is explored to better understand it as a key factor. This exploration was conducted from the existential-humanistic and transpersonal perspective because this truly is the only way to have a full understanding of a human experience such as remorse. Through this, ultimately, the hope was that this study would contribute to understanding not only remorse in the context of restorative justice, but also the potential of this population's experience of remorse to move them to the next level of realization of their potential. This latter goal is also one that complements an intention of restorative justice; to repair harm and relationships and to reintegrate the offender into society in a productive role. Additionally, the importance of this study is that it demonstrates that experiential understanding of remorse is a complex one and, while remorse is used widely in many legal systems, these systems have left this understanding virtually unexplored.

While using the TOSCA-A as an entry point to the more detailed exploration of remorse, its relationship to the ability of the groups or individuals to demonstrate remorse, in many instances was not a direct one. Using these scores to explain or predict the responses was rather a tenuous effort. Sometimes the relationship of the scores to the responses seemed obvious, and others it was difficult to discern, or seemed contradictory. For example, the significantly higher guilt of the high guilt-proneness master study group (see Table 22) compared to the high guilt-proneness pilot group was difficult to explain, as was the significantly higher guilt and lower detachment for the low guilt-proneness master and pilot group comparison (see Table 23). Rather than discounting this tool, the principal investigator believed that it pointed to the complexity of human personality and the different responses that one can get depending upon the individual, the circumstances, and the relationship of the individual to the principal investigator. It does, however, offer some clues and further study might be helpful in broadening the understanding of what this tool can offer. In this commentary, an effort will be made to highlight both the times when the quantitative data of the TOSCA-A reveals a parallel between the qualitative data and the times when it seems to be contradictory.

What could be gleaned from this study as the core of the remorse experience for these adolescents was that, in addition to the guilt felt for harm inflicted, remorse also meant taking responsibility for this harm. It meant feeling, in a very deep empathetic way, the pain of the other or others. It can also have meant feeling the resulting loss, and this loss could be a loss to self, other, or both. These youth viewed remorse as more future-oriented, though it did have a component of being oriented to the past. Lazare (2004) identifies these two qualities of remorse as "backward-facing remorse" and "forward-facing remorse" (p. 108). The former is identification and acknowledgement of harm and the latter he terms forbearance. For the subjects in this study, when oriented toward the future, this meant truly remorseful people made changes in their behavior, and these youth believed those should be lasting changes. Even in this, there was an element of the past, in that the participants did not want to repeat the behavior and re-experience remorse. This relates also to another element of the past, in that they could not disengage from their past, which compelled them to engage in the harmful behavior again.

The most telling information relating to remorse came from the focus groups and the individual case studies. In the focus groups, the inability of the low guilt-proneness groups to sustain the conversation without distracting, externalizing, or deteriorating showed a marked difference between the low and high guilt-proneness groups. This suggested that the guilt-proneness score may well have been a measure of the stability and strength of ego-structure. High guilt-proneness groups were not threatened by the topic and could maintain a cognitive focus on it and needed less coaching and guidance in coming back to topic. They also might have been supported by their ability to take pride in their actions, as indicated by their significantly higher Beta-Pride scores.

In spite of this, all groups provided some level of insight into the experience of remorse for this population. They offered insight into the importance of the internal element of remorse, and that it was clearly not just about external punishments. Though true for both high and low guilt-proneness groups, high guilt-proneness groups presented this in a more positive light as an esteem-building experience, rather than focusing on the pain of the experience as low guilt-proneness groups tended to do. For the most part, their experience was broader than the somatic level that Shafranske (1989) talked about and was more focused on interpersonal and ontological levels of remorse. Additionally, particularly in individual case studies, they were very capable of being empathetic. Both Hoffman (2000) and Gobodo-Madikizela (2002) stress the importance of this in being able to experience remorse and engage in reparative behavior.

They also talked about and struggled with self-love and self-forgiveness. For example, as discussed earlier, both in the pilot study and in the current study, youth expressed a rather unforgiving attitude toward those who re-offend, and these youth do regularly re-offend. They thought that an apology must be accompanied by a change in actions or in how the offender lived his or her life. This might, in Lazare's (2004) terms, be a way of showing that the offender shares and reaffirms the values of the injured person and that safety in their relationship has been restored. They also discussed shame at their homeless circumstance and that help they received from Urban Peak was not something they earned because they were worthy of it, but because people chose to give this to them. This echoes May (1983) in his suggestion that there must be balanced, healthy relationships of self with other, self with humanity, and self with self. Without that balance, one cannot truly understand love. These youth were very much trying to reconcile themselves in these relationships. While more common restorative practices often discuss relationship and harm between two or more people and, in more inclusive processes, the community as well, the existential-humanistic and transpersonal perspective demands that relationship with and harm to self and, in a very deep way, the essence of humanity also carry importance. Focus groups and individual case studies showed that these youth are aware of this importance.

On the other hand, an emergent theme, both in focus groups and in individual case studies, was the factor of something that holds them back from acting in what they view as a more constructive or reparative way. This was stated most poignantly by Steve in his story for Card 3GF and by the male in Group 2. It was tempting to tie this to Tangney's explanation of how shame or guilt mixed with shame operates, but this theme did not seem to relate only to focus groups or individuals with high shame scores or high shame to guilt ratios, nor was it absent in the occurrence of high guilt scores. The most obvious case of this was William, who had guilt and shame scores that were almost equivalent and yet he seemed to have met with the most success by finding and maintaining a job and moving into an apartment. Likewise, Ingrid had almost equivalent guilt and shame scores, both being very high, but she had been unable to sustain a job and move out of the shelter. She was also unable to face her mother and tell her the truth of her situation. While both William and Ingrid were ashamed of their homeless circumstance and both had lied about it, William was able to move himself out of it, while Ingrid was not. One can only guess that, with his high externalization and detachment scores, William's abilities to detach and externalize served him well by allowing him to defend against crippling self attacks and, with UPD's support, to change his situation. In Ingrid's situation, hope might be in pride she had in her artistic abilities. As stated earlier, her pride scores were the highest of the group, she had pride both in herself and in what she accomplished. This was particularly important in that she shared that her father told her she would not amount to much.

Turning now to Steve, the participant who had a shame score that was about half of his guilt score, he fared least well, having lost his services yet again. Most likely he will age out of UPD before being able to successfully make use of UPD's offerings. Linda, who presented with the most stable ego structure, had the lowest shame to guilt ratio, a high guilt score, and pride scores that were both above the mean, was the only one who did not appear stuck in shame, or in her life circumstances. She spoke most about the need to empathize with others and to engage in reparative behavior. While there was no deeply touching story of transformation, Linda did make a huge leap from accepting life in an abusive situation to realizing that this type of treatment was unacceptable for her. This was a leap that many with similar beginnings do not make. Perhaps this was an ongoing transformation with much deeper implications she does not yet fully comprehend. Unfortunately, since she moved on from UPD as soon as she realized it would not meet her needs, what became of her after she left was very much an unknown.

It was interesting that, in comparison to the pilot study group, young people in the subsequent study did not communicate as clear a sense of the transformative power of remorse, though they did still speak about importance of changed behavior as the greatest indicator of true remorse. Also interesting was that this seemed to be a much more internalized experience for them than for the pilot study group. Like the pilot study group, these young people were in the process of becoming. It seemed though that they have expressed a different stage or phase of this process, one that seems much more painful and frustrating than the one that the pilot study group shared. These youth were experiencing the state of being stuck and they spoke more about hopelessness and helplessness than did the pilot study group. Their stories and comments told of a desire to move forward and yet an inexplicable something that kept them from doing so. This was one of the paradoxes which confronted them in their lives.

May (1983) suggested that humans must face these paradoxes in order to attain integration and reach their potential. Their recognition that they continue to repeat past patterns, or to be stuck, places them in the painful dilemma that can be likened, once again, to May's concept of ontological guilt, guilt for their failure to realize their potential. While shame may play into this, Henderson et al.'s (2001) link between shame, fear, and anxiety may offer some insight into a more complex explanation of what keeps these young people from moving toward remorse, reparation, and actualization of their potential. Without courage having been properly nurtured and developed in the difficult circumstances that most of these youth faced in their childhoods, the prospect of facing their fears and experiencing ontological anxiety was intolerable to them. Perhaps what organizations like UPD can do is provide these young people with an environment that meets them where they are in their lives, helps them see the strengths they have in that place, and offers support and encouragement to face fear and anxiety, and move into the future, instead of succumbing to their past.

Existential-Humanistic and Transpersonal Point of View

As was stated previously, a vital part of this study was the opportunity to explore the experience of remorse with these young people from multiple perspectives. The point of doing so was to bring this snapshot to full life, allowing the investigator and readers the opportunity to see a fuller and richer picture of this very human experience. Taken piece by piece, one would not get the same sense of this experience, but by using quantitative measures to offer guidance and entering the phenomenology of this experience with the youth, it brought to light the existential dilemma they faced at this juncture of their lives. Specifically, this was the dilemma of their awareness and desire to move forward that was thwarted by an inexplicable something that kept them from doing so. This paradoxical dilemma truly was the most profound existential finding of this study. Quantitative study alone would not have brought this insight. Further, the principal investigator believed that this insight alone was not likely to bring change, but, it did offer hope that through understanding, assimilation, further work, and support from those who work with this population, growth will come.

One of the most challenging aspects of working with this population is when they become mired in repetitive patterns. The understanding of remorse and its relationship with such repeated patterns can be used to assist them through case management and therapy to move into the "forward-looking remorse," or forbearance. It is also a vital understanding in the use of remorse in the legal system. Before this can be done, however, one has to understand where the youth are in their experience of remorse. It is hoped that this study may offer some process by which that determination can be made. In the spirit of the existential-humanistic and transpersonal tradition, if proper support is offered, then human beings have hope of reaching their potentiality. Because of this, restorative justice and other processes that approach harm with an attitude of reparation rather than punishment hold great promise

for dealing constructively with many of the human behaviors that the legal system seems to be

unable to effectively address.

Treatment and Use of Remorse in the Legal System and Its Literature

This study was initiated due to the ever present and growing importance of remorse in

the processes of restorative justice. Referring back to the dentist in Florida whose lack of

remorse was a factor in his conviction (Goffard, 2002), the seemingly remorseless dog-owner

who faced murder charges, and sentences that are extended when the perpetrator who shows

no remorse, it is easy to see that remorse played and continues to play a critical role in the

outcomes of the legal system.

It is important to reiterate that, while remorse has a pervasive influence in this system,

it is remarkable that description and definition of it is strikingly absent from the literature of

the law. Yet, there are those who argue from a utilitarian stance for an anti-emotion program

in Anglo-American legal system. They suggest that emotions are irrational and, therefore,

should be excluded from consideration (Nussbaum, 2004). Nussbaum argued, however, that

while some emotions can be irrational, they can also be thought-laden and make perfect sense

under the circumstances. This is actually how emotions often can be handled in the system,

but there is very little formal guidance in doing so. Nussbaum also called for a society, and a

legal system, that acknowledges its own inescapable humanity. A further pursuit would be to

seek to explore and have a clearer understanding of human responses such as compassion,

shame, and remorse, including the role they play and how this role might be used

constructively to reach results that are true to both humanity and the spirit of the law.

The importance of remorse in the context of restorative justice does not end with criminal justice. Lazare (2004) writes about the growing importance of sincere and meaningful apologies. He provides examples of apologies in the media, sports, national and international political affairs, and in private relationships between individuals and families. He maintains that these apologies heal and are the beginning of further reparation. This author believes it is obvious that apologies born out of truly remorseful responses can have far-reaching consequences that will make it possible to avoid further animosity and violence both nationally and abroad. Remorse is vitally important to the underpinnings of a sincere and meaningful apology. To reiterate simply and directly the answer to a question of whether or not focus on restorative justice is a valid one, the answer is resoundingly that it is well-founded. The caveat is that it is equally valid that the experience of remorse should be well-understood in order for it to have a more effective, appropriate, and just influence.

REFERENCES

Abrams, D. M. (1999). Six decades of the Bellak scoring system, among others. In L. Gieser & M. I. Stein (Eds.), *Evocative images: The Thematic Apperception Test and the art of projection* (pp. ix-xi). Washington DC: American Psychological Association.

Anderson, J. W. (1999). Murray and the creation of the test. In L. Gieser & M. I. Stein (Eds.), *Evocative images: The Thematic Apperception Test and the art of projection* (pp. 23-38). Washington DC: American Psychological Association.

Bandes, S. A. (1999). Introduction. In S. Bandes (Ed.), *The passions of law* (pp. 1-15). New York: New York University Press.

Bassiouni, M. C. (1993). Human rights in the context of criminal justice: Identifying international procedural protections and equivalent protections in national constitutions. *Duke Journal of Comparative & International Law, 3,* 235-297.

Bazemore, G. (1999). Restorative justice and relational rehabilitation. In G. Bazemore and L. Walgrave (Eds.), *Restorative juvenile justice: Repairing the harm of youth crime* (pp. 155-194). Monsey, NY: Criminal Justice Press.

Bazemore, G., & Walgrave, L. (1999). Introduction: Restorative justice and the international juvenile justice crisis. In G. Bazemore & L. Walgrave (Eds.), *Restorative juvenile justice: Repairing the harm of youth crime* (pp. 1-13). Monsey, NY: Criminal Justice Press.

Bell, J. (2004, January 16). Lack of remorse gets Arvaluk nine months in jail. *Nunatsiaq News.* Retrieved December 25, 2004, from http://www.nunatsiaq.com/archives/40116/news/nunavut/40116_02.html

Bellak, L. (1971). *The T.A.T. and C.A.T. in clinical use* (2nd ed.). New York: Grune & Stratton.

Berk, L. (1994/1991/1989). *Child development* (3rd ed.). Needham Heights, MA: Allyn and Bacon.

Blagg, H. (1997). A just measure of shame? *The British Journal of Criminology, 37*(4), 481-501.

Braithwaite, J. (1989). *Crime, shame, and reintegration.* Cambridge, MA: Cambridge University Press.

Brothers, J. (1989). Remorse and regeneration. In M. Stern (Ed.), *Psychotherapy and the remorseful patient* (pp. 47-62). New York: The Haworth Press.

Bullock, M., & Jones, J. (1999). Beyond surveys: Using focus groups to evaluate university career services. *Journal of Career Planning & Employment, 59*(4), 38-44.

Carter, S. (1988). When victims happen to be black. *Yale Law Journal, 97,* 420-422.

Edington, D. A. (1997). The effects of incarceration on the achievement motivation of African American males. *The Berkeley McNair Journal, 5.* Retrieved March 3, 2003, from http://www-mcnair.berkeley.edu/97journal/Edington.html

Endicott, O. (2001, January). *Analysis of the Supreme Court of Canada's decision in the Latimer murder case.* Retrieved February 23, 2003, from http://www.acl.on.ca/latimer/analysis.html

Erikson, E. H. (1950/1963/1985). *Childhood and society* (35th anniversary ed.). New York: W.W. Norton.

Faure, G. O. (1995). Conflict formulation: Going beyond culture-bound views of conflict. In B. B. Bunker & J. Z. Rubin (Eds.), *Conflict cooperation and justice* (pp. 39-57). San Francisco: Jossey-Bass.

Federal Sentencing Guideline Manual. (2002a, November 1). *Sentencing table.* Retrieved March 16, 2003, from http://www.ussc.gov/2002guid/TABCON02.html

Federal Sentencing Guideline Manual. (2002b, November 1). Acceptance of responsibility. In *Adjustments* (chap. 3). Retrieved March 16, 2003, from http://www.ussc.gov/2002guid/TABCON02.html

Ferguson, T. J., & Stegge, H. (1998). Measuring guilt in children: A rose by any other name still has thorns. In J. Bybee (Ed.), *Guilt and children* (pp. 19-74). San Diego, CA: Academic Press.

Gilbert, P., & Gilbert, J. (2003). Entrapment and arrested fight and flight in depression: An exploration using focus groups. *Psychology and Psychotherapy, 76,* 173.

Gobodo-Madikizela, P. (2002). Remorse, forgiveness, and rehumanization: Stories from South Africa. *Journal of Humanistic Psychology, 42,* 7-32.

Goffard, C. (2002, November 21). Lack of remorse played heavily against doctor. *St. Petersburg Times.* Retrieved December 25, 2004, from http://www.sptimes.com/2002/11/21/TampaBay/Lack_of_remorse_playe.shtml

Gould, W. (2002, March 13). Report: Lack of remorse hurt dog-mauling defendants. *CBS-5 Eyewitness News.* Retrieved December 25, 2004, from http://cbs5.com/ news/local/2002/03/14/Report:_Lack_of_Remorse_Hurt_Dog-Mauling_ Defendants.html

Greenberg, G,. & Fitzpatrick, M. (1989). The significance of remorse in psychotherapy. In M. Stern (Ed.), *Psychotherapy and the remorseful patient* (pp. 35-46). New York: The Haworth Press.

Greene, J. C., Caracelli, V. J., & Graham, W. F. (1989). Toward a conceptual framework for mixed-method evaluation designs. *Educational and Evaluation Policy Analysis, 11*(3), 255-274.

Harder, D. W. & Zalma, A. (1990). Two promising shame and guilt scales: A construct validity comparison. *Journal of Personality Assessment, 5*, 729-745.

Harris, J. R. (1999). *The nurture assumption: Why children turn out the way they do.* New York: Simon and Schuster.

Hauck, P. (1989). The remorseful patient. In M. Stern (Ed.), *Psychotherapy and the remorseful patient* (pp. 13-16). New York: The Haworth Press.

Henderson, L., Zimbardo, P., & Martinez, A. (2001). *Social fitness training, restructuring self-blaming attributions and reducing shame: Preliminary data.* (The Shyness Institute). Stanford, CA: Stanford University.

Hoffman, M. (2000). *Empathy and moral development: Implications for caring and justice.* Cambridge: Cambridge University Press.

Hoffman, M. (1998). Varieties of empathy-based guilt. In J. Bybee (Ed.), *Guilt and children* (pp. 91-112). San Diego, CA: Academic Press.

Houston, J. (1987). *The search for the beloved.* Los Angeles: Jeremy P. Tarcher.

Immarigeon, R. (1999). Restorative justice, juvenile offenders and crime victims: A review of the literature. In G. Bazemore & L. Walgrave (Eds.), *Restorative juvenile justice: Repairing the harm of youth crime* (pp. 305-326). Monsey, NY: Criminal Justice Press.

Jacobsen, B., & Theilgaard, A. (1999). Kierkegaard and remorse: Remorse is an existential concern. In M. Cox (Ed.), *Remorse and reparation* (pp. 189-199). London: Jessica Kingsley.

Johnson, T. (2002). *In African American males in the criminal justice system.* Retrieved January 31, 2003, from http://www.co.hennepin.mn.us/opd/Reports/AAmenproject/jan2002/researchcompendium/Howaretheylivingtheirlives/6chapter2.html

Kaplan R. M., & Saccuzzo, D. P. (1997). *Psychological testing: Principles, applications, and issues.* Pacific Grove, CA: Brooks/Cole.

Karen, R. (2001, June 10). Commentary: Seeing McVeigh as the "Other" costs us our own humanity. *The Los Angeles Times*, p. M.5.

Kaufman, G. (1980/1985). Shame: The power of caring. Cambridge, MA: Schenkman Books.

Keeva, S. (1999). Does law mean never having to say you're sorry? *American Bar Association Journal, 85*, 64-68.

Kierkegaard, S. A. (1990). *Judge for yourself.* (H. V. Hong & E. H. Hong, Trans.). Princeton, NJ: Princeton University Press. (Original work published 1851)

Kierkegaard, S. A. (1980). *The concept of anxiety.* (R. Thomte & A. B. Anderson, Trans.). Princeton, NJ: Princeton University Press. (Original work published 1844)

Kolb, D. M., & Coolidge, G. G. (1991). Her place at the table: A consideration of gender issues in negotiation. In J. W. Breslin, W. Breslin, & J. Z. Rubin (Eds.), *Negotiation: Theory and practice* (pp. 267-277). Boston: Harvard Law School Program on Negotiation.

Krueger, R. A., & Casey, M. A. (2000). *Focus groups: A practical guide for applied research* (3rd ed.). Thousand Oaks, CA: Sage.

Lazare, A. (2004). *On apology.* New York: Oxford University Press.

Lederach, J. P. (1992). *Beyond prescription: New lenses for conflict resolution training across cultures.* Unpublished manuscript, Conrad Grebel College, Waterloo, Ontario, Canada.

Lukoff, D., & Edwards, D. (1996/2000). *Case study methods in psychology.* (Learning Guide, Course No. 1140). San Francisco: Saybrook Graduate School and Research Center.

Maslow, A. H. (1971). *The farther reaches of human nature.* New York: Penguin Books.

May, R. (1983). *The discovery of being.* New York: W. W. Norton.

Marshall, T. (1996). Criminal mediation in Great Britain 1980-1996. *European Journal on Criminal Policy and Research, 4*(4), 21-43.

Massaro, T. (1991). Shame, culture, and American criminal law. *Michigan Law Review, 89*, 1880-1944.

McClelland, D. C. (1999). How the test lives on: Extensions of the Thematic Apperception approach. In L. Gieser & M. I. Stein (Eds.), *Evocative images: The Thematic Apperception Test and the art of projection* (pp. 163-176). Washington DC: American Psychological Association.

Moeser, J. P. (1999). Reclaiming juvenile justice for the 21st century: Balanced and restorative justice. *Reclaiming Children and Youth, 8*(3), 162-168.

138

Moore, T. (1989). Remorse: An initiatory disturbance of the soul. In E. M. Stern (Ed.), *Psychotherapy and the remorseful patient* (pp. 83-94). New York: The Haworth Press.

Morgan, C. D. & Murray, H. A. (1935). A method for investigating fantasies: The Thematic Apperception Test. *Archives of Neurological Psychiatry, 34,* 289-306.

Morgan, D. L. (1997). *Focus groups as qualitative research* (2nd ed.). Thousand Oaks, CA: Sage.

Morrison, A. (1989). *Shame: The underside of narcissism.* Hillsdale, NJ: The Analytic Press.

Murray, C. (1999). Foreword: Harry's compass. In L. Gieser & M. I. Stein (Eds.), *Evocative images: The Thematic Apperception Test and the art of projection* (pp. ix-xi). Washington DC: American Psychological Association.

Nader, L., & Combs-Schilling, E. (1977). Restitution in cross-cultural perspective. In J. Hudson & B. Galaway (Eds.), *Restitution in criminal justice.* Lexington, MA: Lexington Books.

Nussbaum, M. C. (2004). *Hiding from humanity: Disgust, shame, and the law.* Princeton, NJ: Princeton University Press.

Piaget, J. (1932/1965). *The moral judgment of the child.* New York: Norton.

Reynolds, H. (1989). *Dispossession: Black Australia and white invaders.* Sydney, Australia: Allen and Unwin.

Rosenzweig, S. (1999). Pioneer experiences in the clinical development of the Thematic Apperception Test. In L. Gieser & M. I. Stein (Eds.), *Evocative images: The Thematic Apperception Test and the art of projection* (pp. ix-xi). Washington DC: American Psychological Association.

Said, E. (1995). *Orientalism: Western conceptions of the Orient.* Harmondsworth, Middlesex, United Kingdom: Penguin.

Sanchez, R. (2005, February 13). A family's forgiveness. *The Denver Post,* pp. A1, A19.

Sarat, A. (1999). Remorse, responsibility, and criminal justice: An analysis of popular culture. In S. Bandes (Ed.), *The passions of law* (pp. 168-190). New York: New York University Press.

Scheper-Hughes, N. (1999). The undoing: Social suffering and the politics of remorse. In M. Cox (Ed.), *Remorse and reparation* (pp. 145-170). London: Jessica Kingsley Publishers.

139

Schiff, M. (1999). The impact of restorative interventions on juvenile offenders. In G. Bazemore & L. Walgrave (Eds.), *Restorative juvenile justice: Repairing the harm of youth crime* (pp. 327-356). Monsey, NY: Criminal Justice Press.

Schneider, A. L. (1990). *Deterrence and juvenile crime.* New York: Springer-Verlag.

Schneidman, E. S. (1999). The Thematic Apperception Test: A paradise of psychodynamics. In L. Gieser & M. I. Stein (Eds.), *Evocative images: The Thematic Apperception Test and the art of projection* (pp. 87-105). Washington DC: American Psychological Association.

Shafranske, E.P. (1989). The significance of remorse in psychotherapy. In E. M. Stern (Ed.), *Psychotherapy and the remorseful patient* (pp. 19-34). New York: The Haworth Press.

Sharpe, S. (1998). *Restorative justice: A vision for healing and change.* Edmonton, Alberta, Canada: Edmonton Victim Offender Mediation Society.

Shaw, J. (1989). The usefulness of remorse. In E. M. Stern (Ed.), *Psychotherapy and the remorseful patient* (pp. 77-82). New York: The Haworth Press.

Smith, R. (1988). The logic and design of case study research. *The Sport Psychologist, 2,* 1-12.

Spencer, W. (2004). *Spencer on existential psychology.* Eastern Illinois University. Retrieved November 21, 2004, from http://oldsci.eiu.edu/psychology/Spencer /Existential.html

Stern, M. (1989). The psychotherapy of remorse. In M. Stern (Ed.), *Psychotherapy and the remorseful patient* (pp. 1-12). New York: The Haworth Press.

Tangney, J. P., & Dearing, R. L. (2002). *Shame and guilt.* New York: The Guilford Press.

Tangney, J. P., Wagner P., & Gramzow, R. (1992). Proneness to shame, proneness to guilt, and psychopathology. *Journal of Abnormal Psychology, 101*(3), 469-478.

Tangney, J. P. (1991). Moral affect: The good, the bad, and the ugly. *Journal of Personality and Social Psychology, 61,* 598-607.

Teglasi, H. (2001). *Essentials of TAT and other storytelling techniques assessment.* New York: Wiley.

Tillich, P. (1952). *The courage to be.* New Haven, CT: Yale University Press.

Tomkins, S. (1995). *Shame and its sisters: A Silvan Tomkins reader.* Durham, NC: Duke University Press.

Twohig, P. L., & Putnam, W. (2002). Group interviews in primary care research: Advancing the state of the art of ritualized research? *Family Practice, 19*(3), 278-284.

Umbreit, M., Coates, R., & Vos, B. (2001). Victim impact of meeting with young offenders: Two decades of victim offender mediation practice and research. In A. Morris & G. Maxwell (Eds.), *Restorative justice for juveniles: Conferencing, mediation and circles* (pp. 121-143). Portland, OR: Hart.

Van Ness, D. (1999). Legal issues of restorative justice. In G. Bazemore & L. Walgrave (Eds.), *Restorative juvenile justice: Repairing the harm of youth crime* (pp. 263-284). Monsey, NY: Criminal Justice Press.

Van Ness, D., Morris, A., & Maxwell, G. (2001). Introducing restorative justice. In A. Morris & G. Maxwell (Eds.), *Restorative justice for juveniles: Conferencing, mediation and circles* (pp. 3-12). Portland, OR: Hart.

Vasquez, G. (2000). Resiliency: Juvenile offenders recognize their strengths to change their lives. *Corrections Today, 62*(3), 106-116.

Weitekamp, E. G. (1999). The history of restorative justice. In G. Bazemore & L. Walgrave (Eds.), *Restorative juvenile justice: Repairing the harm of youth crime* (pp. 75-102). Monsey, NY: Criminal Justice Press.

Werner, E., & Smith, R. (1992). Overcoming the odds: High-risk children from birth to adulthood. Ithaca, NY: Cornell University Press.

Westen, D. (1998). The scientific legacy of Sigmund Freud: Toward a psychodynamically informed psychological science. *Psychological Bulletin, 124*(3), 333-371.

World Congress of Youth. (2000). *Frequently asked questions.* Retrieved September 22, 2002, from http://www.wcyunited.org/questions_and_answers.html

Young, R. (2001). Just cops doing "shameful" business?: Police-led restorative justice and the lessons of research. In A. Morris & G. Maxwell (Eds.), *Restorative justice for juveniles: Conferencing, mediation and circles* (pp. 196-226). Portland, OR: Hart.

Zehr, H. (1990). *Changing lenses: A new focus for crime and justice.* Scottdale, PA: Herald Press.

APPENDIX A - CONSENT TO PARTICIPATE IN RESEARCH

Purpose:
The purpose of this research is to gain understanding of the construct of remorse as it applies to adolescents between the ages of 18 and 21 who are in at-risk situations. This project is being conducted by Gigi Higgins, a graduate student of Saybrook Graduate School and Research Center, as part of dissertation research.

Principal Investigator:
Gigi Higgins
730 21st Street, Denver, CO 80205
303-777-9198 x251, e-mail: gigi.higgins@urbanpeak.org

Procedures:
[1] This study involves filling out one questionnaire and possible participation in a focus group. Additionally, some participants will be asked to take part in follow-up individual case studies. These case studies will involve completion of a second questionnaire, completion of a projective test, and review of case history and case notes.
[2] Instruction and completion of the questionnaire will take twenty to thirty minutes. Participation in the focus group will take one hour. The total time for those participants doing both will be one hour and thirty minutes. Participation in the case studies will require two additional sessions of approximately one hour each per participant.
[3] The questionnaire is a self-report tool containing 15 scenarios with 4 or 5 responses for which you will be asked to rate the likelihood of each response on a scale from 1 to 5, 1 being "not at all likely" and 5 being "very likely." The focus group is a guided group discussion and includes 2-3 other participants. The discussion is tape-recorded. It will be led by Gigi Higgins, and will cover a set of questions on the topic of remorse for which your opinions and comments on those of other participants are requested.
[5] For the case study, the second questionnaire is a list of 22 feelings that are to be ranked on a scale from 0 to 4 (0 being not experienced at all and 4 being experienced continuously). The projective test consists of administering a set of 16 of the pictures from the standard Thematic Apperception Test cards. Participants will be asked to tell a story about each picture. Participants will have an opportunity to discuss any thoughts or concerns about the tests at the end of each session.

Possible Risks and Safeguards:
This study is designed to minimize as much as possible any potential psychological and social risks to you. Although very unlikely, there are always risks in research, which you are entitled to know in advance of giving your consent, as well as the safeguards to be taken by those who conduct the project to minimize the risks.

I understand that:
1. My participation will not have any bearing on my services at Urban Peak, or any affiliated agency from which I receive services, with the exception that, upon my authorization, I may receive one life skills credit for my participation.
2. Although my identity will be known to the principal investigator and possibly other staff at Urban Peak, all identifying information shall be removed from the questionnaire and at the time of transcription of tape recordings from the focus group and case studies.
3. My responses to the questions will be pooled with others and all identifiers or related information that might be used to identify me, will be given a number or pseudonym.
4. This consent form will be kept separate from the data I provide, in a locked box for three years, known only to the principal investigator, after which it too will be destroyed.

5. The data collected in its raw and transcribed forms are to be kept anonymous, stored in a locked container accessible only to the principal investigator for three years, after which it will be destroyed. The dissertation chair, Dr. Eugene Taylor will be advised of its location should the principal investigator pass away unexpectedly before the three years expire.
6. Transcribed data in the form of computer disks containing anonymous spreadsheets and anonymous response listings from all participants to each question will be kept indefinitely for future research.
7. All the information I give will be kept confidential to the extent permitted by law. The information I provide will be examined in terms of group findings, and will be reported anonymously.
8. There is to be no individual feedback regarding my test scores or interpretations of my responses. Only general findings will be presented in a Summary Report of which I am entitled a copy, and my individual responses are to remain anonymous.
9. All personal information I provide regarding my identity will not be released to any other party, outside of appropriate Urban Peak staff, without my explicit written permission.
10. I will be known to other participants in the focus group and therefore, to uphold the confidentiality of the research, I shall not discuss the contents of my focus group with others outside the focus group in any way which might identify the other participants.
11. If quotes of my responses are used in the research report for the course, as well as any and all future publications of these quotations, my identity shall remain anonymous, and at most make use of a fictitious name.
12. I have the right to refuse to answer any question asked of me.
13. I have the right to refuse at any time to engage in any procedure requested of me.
14. I have the right to withdraw from participation at any time for any reason without stating my reason.
15. I have the right to participate without prejudice on the part of the principal investigator.
16. It is possible that the procedures may bring to my mind thoughts of an emotional nature that may upset me. In the unlikely event that I become upset or experience emotional distress from my participation, the principal investigator shall be available to me. She will make every effort to minimize such an occurrence. However, if an upset occurs and becomes sufficiently serious to warrant professional attention, as a condition of my participation in this study, I understand my case manager can assist with this or arrange for referral to a therapist. I am also aware that if the investigator has any serious concerns of this nature, she will discuss this with me and encourage me to talk with my case manager and that the investigator will alert my case manager to a possible issue, as is allowed by the release I have signed with Urban Peak.
17. By my consent, I understand I must notify the principal investigator at the time of any serious emotional upset that may cause me to seek therapy and compensation for this upset.

Regarding any concern and serious upset, you may contact the principal investigator at: 303-777-9198 X251. You may also contact the Research Supervisor of the project, Dr. Eugene Taylor by phone at 617-492-1130 or e-mail at etaylor@saybrook.edu. Should you have any concerns regarding the conduct and procedures of this research project that are not addressed to your satisfaction by the principal investigator and his or her research supervisor, you may report and discuss them with Dr. Arne Collen the Chair of the Saybrook Institutional Review Board at: 925-930-9779 or acollen@saybrook.edu.

Benefits:
I understand that my participation in this study may have possible and potential benefits.
[1] I may obtain a greater personal awareness, knowledge, and understanding of remorse.
[2] Through future communications and possible applications of the findings of the research, indirectly my participation may bring future benefits to others who may become involved in the restorative justice process.

143

[3] My participation may enable the principal investigator and others working in the topic area to make a contribution to knowledge and theory of remorse as it is used in the restorative justice process.

Summary Report:
Upon conclusion of this study, a summary report of the general findings will become available. If you would like a copy of the report, please check below.

___ Yes, I would like a copy of the report.

Disclaimer:
Participation in this study puts participants at some psychological and social risks, but not physical risks. Saybrook Graduate School and Research Center will not provide compensation or medical care in the unlikely event it can be established that injuries are incurred as a result of participation in this research project.

Consent of Principal Investigator:
I have explained the above procedures and conditions to this study, and provided an opportunity for the research participant to ask questions and have attempted to provide satisfactory answers to all questions that have been asked in the course of this explanation.

_____
Signature   Date

_____
Print name

Consent of the Participant:
If you have any questions of the principal investigator at this point, please take this opportunity to have them answered before granting your consent. If you are ready to provide your consent, read the statement below, then sign, and print your name and date on the line below.

I have read the above information, have had an opportunity to ask questions about any and all aspects of this study, and give my voluntary consent to participate.

_____
Signature   Date

_____
Print name

APPENDIX B – PROTOCOL FOR FOCUS GROUPS

The members of the groups will most likely be familiar with each other. In this case, there will be no need for introductions. If this is not the case, brief introductions will be made and each person will be asked to share something about themselves, like their favorite food. If there is an assistant in the group in addition to the principal investigator, the roles of the facilitator and assistant will be briefly described. Once this has been done, the script will go as follows:

The topic of today's discussion is one that relates to a process that several of you may be familiar with. This process is restorative or reparative justice. Would anyone who is familiar with this process like to tell us your understanding of how this process works? Depending upon how the group responds, the principal investigator will fill in or provide the explanation as follows: *Restorative or reparative justice is a process in which someone (or a group of people) who has experienced some loss or harm due to the actions of another can meet and talk with the person or persons responsible for these actions. In talking about the situation, those who have been harmed have the opportunity to talk about the effects of those actions. The person(s) responsible for the actions may talk about the reason for the actions and the thoughts and events that led up to those actions. The participants in this restorative meeting will usually create an agreement stating what action the responsible person or persons will take as a way of repairing the harm that was done.*

Following this description, the script continued as follows:

Something that often comes up in choosing to use this process, and during the process itself, is whether or not the person who did the harmful actions feels remorse for the harm that was done. As someone who has led the process of restorative justice, I have been in the position of deciding whether or not someone feels remorse. In trying to make this decision about participants who are young people similar to yourselves, the question for me was how does this look, sound, and feel for them and for you? This research is based on my belief that this is an important question for helping people who use restorative justice to have a better understanding of young people who may be participants in this process.

Two questions I would like to explore today are: 1) What is your experience when you have harmed someone or something and you feel badly about that?; and 2) What behavior would you look for from someone who had harmed you in order for you to feel that this person had remorse for what he or she had done ? In your discussion of both questions, include how it looks, what words might be said, how it sounds (voice tone, etc.), and how it might feel from an emotional perspective.

As discussed in the informed consent form that you signed previously, this session will last one hour and it will be tape-recorded. I ask that you try to speak one at a time and if there are several people who have thoughts they want to share I will help facilitate this so everyone has a chance to speak. Let's also remember that in the informed consent form, each of you agreed to maintain confidentiality and will not discuss the contents of my focus group with others outside the focus group in any way that might identify the other participants. You may also end your participation in this group at any time that you feel that you need to do so.

In order to start thinking about our topic, I would like each of you to begin by thinking about words that come to your mind that describe remorse. Write them down on the paper you have been provided. Then we will be begin by moving around the room asking each one of you to briefly share a thought you have about what you think remorse is, perhaps something from your paper. From there we will move into a general discussion about the two questions I have listed.

The remainder of this group will be structured by the discussion of the group members with guiding and probing questions from the primary investigator as appropriate.

APPENDIX C – PERSONAL FEELINGS QUESTIONNAIRE - - 2
D. W. Harder

For each of the following listed feelings, to the left of the item number, please place a number from 0 to 4, reflecting how common the feeling is for you.

A "4" means that you experience the feeling continuously or almost continuously.
A "3" means that you experience the feeling frequently but not continuously.
A "2" means that you experience the feeling some of the time.
A "1" means that you experience the feeling rarely.
A "0" means that you never experience the feeling.

_____ 1.   Embarrassment

_____ 2.   mild guilt

_____ 3.   feeling ridiculous

_____ 4.   worry about hurting or injuring someone

_____ 5.   sadness

_____ 6.   self-conscious

_____ 7.   feeling humiliated

_____ 8.   intense guilt

_____ 9.   euphoria

_____ 10. feeling "stupid"

_____ 11. regret

_____ 12. feeling "childish"

_____ 13. mild happiness

_____ 14. feeling helpless, paralyzed

_____ 15. depression

_____ 16. feelings of blushing

_____ 17. feeling you deserve criticism for what you did

_____ 18. feeling laughable

_____ 19. rage

_____ 20. enjoyment

_____ 21. feeling disgusting to others

_____ 22. remorse

APPENDIX D – TAT SCORING SPREADSHEET

	Card 1		. . . Card #N	Summary
Main Theme				
Main Hero(ine) Age, gender, vocation, abilities, interests, traits, body image, adequacy, self-image				
Remorse Sense of wanting to have done something differently or to undo it				
Empathy Ability to sense other's feelings, experience, thoughts				
Shame Expressions of an intrinsically unworthy or bad self, wanting to hide				
Guilt Taking responsibility for an action or behavior that one regrets				
Parental Relationships Parental interactions as they either support in gaining empathy/feeling empowered or in blaming/ feeling shamed				
Anger Type of anger – direct, constructive or blaming, vengeful				
Blaming Projection of responsibility for bad behaviors onto others or to bad self				
Externalization Projection of bad behaviors onto external environment				
Desire for Reparation Seeking ways to fix harm or alleviate bad feelings caused by hero(ine)				

Printed in the United States
131959LV00003B/16/A

9 783836 428415